Taylor Swift

SECRETS OF A SONGWRITER

AMY GAIL HANSEN

TRIUMPH
BOOKS

This book is available in quantity at special discounts for your group or organization. For further
information, contact:

Triumph Books
542 South Dearborn Street
Suite 750
Chicago, Illinois 60605
(312) 939-3330
Fax (312) 663-3557
www.triumphbooks.com

Printed in U.S.A.
ISBN: 978-1-60078-429-3

Design and page production by Andrew Burwell
Project Management by Rockett Media

Cover design and additional page production by Paul Petrowsky

Taylor Swift:
Secrets of a Songwriter

INTRODUCTION

The *Associated Press* named her Entertainer of the Year in 2009. According to *Billboard*, her sophomore album *Fearless* was the best selling album that same year. And she's the top-selling digital artist in music history, with tons of awards and No. 1 songs under her belt. Oh, and she's 20 years old.

Who is this music superstar? None other than country singer turned pop music princess, singer-songwriter Taylor Swift.

Taylor has definitely earned the title of songwriter. After all, Taylor has written or co-written every song on both her self-titled and *Fearless* albums. Songwriting is what sets her apart from other musicians of any age. She's the ultimate multitasker; she sings, plays guitar and piano, and writes songs. Fans young and old cherish her thought-provoking lyrics about relationships, break ups, first dates, and the power of change.

In the first book of this series, *Taylor Swift: Love Story*, fans learned Taylor's life story—from her childhood to her "swift" rise to fame, from boyfriends to best friends. *Taylor Swift: Secrets of a Songwriter* takes off where that first book left off. It's an exploration of Taylor's songwriting genius, from an analysis of her lyrics to an introduction to her songwriting partners, from her blogs and journals to a support system made up of family and friends. This book explores the people, places, things, moments, and events that have catapulted this songwriter to her throne as princess of the music industry.

So, how did Taylor get her start in music? What pivotal moments of her childhood shaped her into the gifted singer-songwriter she is today? Music was a part of Taylor's life, even as baby. "[My] mom says she remembers folding clothes as I lay in my crib, just a few months old, and I started softly cooing," Taylor recalled. "She called my dad in, and they were convinced that I was singing to them." *Chapter One: Falling in Love with Words* mines Taylor's past for the turning points in her musical life. This chapter shows how her early passion for writing and poetry, coupled with theater and karaoke experiences, propelled her to choose music as a career. It also illustrates the power of positive thinking and provides Taylor's best tips for aspiring singer-songwriters.

Songwriting is something Taylor latched onto after realizing she was one of many girls who could sing.

"I didn't want to just be another girl singer," Taylor said. "I wanted there to be something that set me apart. And I knew that had to be my writing." Songwriting is the strength of both of her albums, as well as her special edition LPs. *Chapter Two: Introducing Taylor Swift* and *Chapter Three: Fearless is Fabulous* take you into the heart and soul of Taylor's music: her lyrics. Every Taylor Swift song has a backstory, and every story is included in these chapters. Creative writing techniques, like similes and metaphors, are uncovered, as well as motifs, rhyme schemes, and allusions.

Taylor loves to write her own songs, but she also loves to share the songwriting process. She's written with some talented songwriters, like Liz Rose, John Rich and Colbie Caillat. *Chapter Four: Taylor Puts the "T" in Teamwork* tells you more about these collaborators and uncovers how Taylor has used teamwork to enhance her career.

Of course, Taylor doesn't limit herself to songwriting; she also writes extensively on her MySpace blog, journals, and even Twitter. Taylor is so fond of stationery and letter writing, she partnered with a major greeting card company to produce her own line of cards. *Chapter Five: Beyond Lyrics: Taylor's Blogs, Journals and More* illustrates how Taylor uses informal writing to not only keep in touch with fans, but also build creative writing partnerships.

Taylor is very competitive; her dedication and love of music have driven her success. But her family, friends, business partners, and fans keep her going strong. Taylor relies on many people to support and encourage her, as well as keep her grounded. *Chapter Six: People and Places* explores not only the people in Taylor's life but the places that have inspired her songwriting and her creativity.

Keeping up with Taylor Swift is a challenge; she's constantly making headlines and doing something new. Want the latest Taylor news? Check out *Chapter Seven: What's Up, Taylor?* It has the most current Taylor Swift facts, from how she celebrated her 20th birthday to the 2010 Grammys to her motion-picture acting debut in *Valentine's Day*. Plus, find out more about her short and highly publicized relationship with Taylor Lautner and what's next for Taylor in the boyfriends department, the second leg of her *Fearless* Tour, her new home, and her third album.

No matter what the future holds, songwriting will always be the outlet for Taylor's emotion, and her connection to the world. She knows the real secret of songwriting. "I absolutely can't stop writing songs," she told *Rolling Stone*. "It's funny because sometimes you'll hear artists talking about how they have to hurry up and write this next record and it's like, I can't stop writing. I can't turn it off. I go through situations, and I go through experiences, and I go through life, and I need to write it…It's like breathing."

Spoken like a true songwriter.

Chapter One

Falling in Love with Words

CHAPTER ONE: Falling in Love with Words

Are songwriters born or made? In other words, do you come into the world with a natural talent to pair words with music, or is it a skill you learn only over time? If the songwriter is Taylor Swift, then the answer is, a little bit of both.

It's clear Taylor has loved words and music from a very young age, and she began expressing her creativity in writing and music during childhood. But she also learned many lessons along the way, lessons that both inspired her to succeed and encouraged her to master the craft of songwriting. There were movies, songs, television programs, role models, and teachers that helped shape Taylor Swift into the music sensation she is today. For all the time spent daydreaming and wishing she'd one day be a star, there were times of sadness, confusion, and frustration. Her story is made up of moments both small and big, both happy and sad, that changed the course of her life.

Once Upon a Time

Taylor's story begins on December 13, 1989, in Wyomissing, Pennsylvania, a small, wealthy suburb of Reading. Her parents, Andrea and Scott Swift, named their daughter Taylor because they thought an androgynous name would prove helpful in the business world. "My mom thought it was cool that if you got a business card that said 'Taylor,' you wouldn't know if it was a guy or a girl," explained Taylor, whose middle name honors her aunt, Alison.

In some ways, Taylor's childhood was like a page out of a fairy tale. She grew up on an 11-acre Christmas tree farm, where she owned horses and cats. Her father, a stockbroker with Merrill Lynch, commuted to the city each day for work, but would return home to do chores on the farm, like building a split-rail fence. Taylor's mom stayed home to care for Taylor and her younger brother, Austin.

"I couldn't have asked for more from my childhood," Taylor told *Glamour*. "My mom quit working when I was four, so she was always around, and my dad is just hilarious." Living on a farm had its advantages. Taylor enjoyed having "all this space to run around, and the [freedom] to be a crazy kid with tangled hair."

As a child, Taylor was fascinated by storytelling. She often begged her parents to read or tell her bedtime stories every night. "I think I fell in love with words before I fell in love with music," she said. "All I wanted to do was talk and all I wanted to do was hear stories."

Taylor's parents noticed her love of words and music early on. When she was just three years old, her parents took her to see Disney's *The Little Mermaid*. "On the way home from seeing that movie in the theaters, I was in the car in the back seat singing the words to the songs I'd heard in the movie," Taylor explained to *The New York Times Style Magazine*. "And they kind of looked at each other and were really confused as to how I was remembering the words after seeing the movie only once."

Looking back on this memory, Taylor realized her interest in music was innate, something borne inside her. "I think that was my first real comprehension of the fact that music was what I remember the most from a movie," she said. "Not exactly the plotline as much as the music."

Contemporary rock music also played an important role in shaping Taylor's musical abilities. Although her mother wasn't musically inclined, she was "obsessed" with Def Leppard, and she listened to the band's music while she was pregnant. Taylor grew up listening to to her mom's music; Def Leppard songs, like "Photograph" and "Hysteria" are the melodies of her childhood.

Taylor probably inherited her musical abilities from her maternal grandmother, Marjorie Finlay, who was an international opera singer and recording star in Puerto Rico. While her grandfather engineered oil rigs overseas, her grandmother starred in *The Bartered Bride, The Barber of Seville,* and *West Side Story*. Taylor fondly recalls listening to her grandmother sing around the house and every Sunday at church, where Taylor watched these performances from her church pew.

"I think watching her get up in front of people every single week made me think it wasn't that big of a deal to get up in front of people," explained Taylor, who still cherishes a set of glamorous black and white photos of her grandmother.

"Blue"

The biggest musical inspiration moment of Taylor's early childhood, though, was hearing the song "Blue" by LeAnn Rimes. When Taylor first heard it at age six, she fell in love with country music. "That song just completely resonated with me. I think what resonated with me even more was that she [LeAnn] was young, and she was doing these things I could only dream about doing," explained Taylor. "All the things that I would daydream

LeAnn's Advice
for Taylor

■ Taylor remembers listening to LeAnn Rimes as a child, and even attending her concerts. But is it possible that LeAnn Rimes remembers Taylor Swift? Absolutely.

"It's so funny, she used to come to my concerts when she was really little, and of course I was very young too," LeAnn explained to Dial-Global, according to *GAC TV.* "She would be one of those little girls in the front row who was raising her hands and just wanting to touch me and wanting to sing with me, and it was adorable. So, that's how I remember her—as this tiny little girl coming to my shows."

LeAnn climbed the charts with her song "Blue" when she was just 14 years old and had to grow up in the spotlight of being a country music singer. So, what advice would she give Taylor Swift? "Be a kid. This whole life is here and it can wait," she said. "Have fun being a child and then, eventually, when you kind of have a bit of a grasp on it, as an adult, then go after it."

This isn't the way Taylor has approached her career, though. Instead, Taylor hit the music industry head on since she was 16, even headlining a tour at age 19. Taylor seems to embrace the fact that she's young. "I actually love it when they come up with some statistic that I was the youngest to do this or the youngest to do that… Honestly, when I was younger, I thought that I was going to be in college studying business when I was 19," she said. "I didn't think that I would get to look back on these last couple of years of my life and see all of these award show moments flash by… I feel very lucky that these things have happened to me at a young age."

about in my bedroom she was up there doing, and she was 14 years old, and I thought there was something so motivating about that."

Once Taylor brought home LeAnn Rimes' album *Blue,* which included other hits like "The Light in Your Eyes" and "Hurt Me," she was hooked on country music. "I started listening to female country artists nonstop: Faith Hill, Shania Twain, the Dixie Chicks. And they led me back to Patsy Cline (for whom the song "Blue" was originally written) and Loretta Lynn and Tammy Wynette," Taylor told *Blender.* "I think it was the storytelling that really grabbed me."

Country singer LeAnn Rimes remembers seeing a young Taylor Swift in the front row of her concerts.

Taylor also loved to read. Her favorites as a young child were Dr. Seuss and the humorous poetry of Shel Silverstein. She immediately connected with poetry as an art form. "I noticed early on that poetry was something that just stuck in my head, and I was replaying those rhymes and try to think of my own," she told *Rolling Stone.* "In English, the only thing I wanted to do was poetry and all the other kids were like, 'Oh, man. We have to write poems again?' and I would have a three-page long poem."

In fourth grade, Taylor was so gifted at poetry, she entered her original three-page poem, "Monster in My Closet," in a national poetry contest and won first place. "Yeah, that was big time," Taylor said years later, proudly looking back on the honor. She was also selected as one of the top ten poetry writers in Pennsylvania, which led to her poems appearing in an anthology. Winning the contest and getting published gave Taylor confidence in her writing abilities. "I found I could make words bounce off the page," she said.

Not long after her poetry prize, Taylor also started performing in musicals. She played Sandy in *Grease,* Kim in *Bye, Bye Birdie,* as well as the parts of Louisa and Maria in two different productions of *The Sound of Music.* She

During her *Fearless* Tour, Taylor sang a duet with John Mayer, a fellow musician who also writes his own songs.

Since childhood, Taylor has possessed a strong stage presence. In December 2009, she lit up the stage with Martin Johnson of Boys Like Girls at the Z100 Jingle Ball.

also performed in a production of *Annie*. Taylor was first bit by the acting bug in second grade after appearing in a school play.

"I knew I wanted to act and sing when I was in that play," Taylor recalled. "Right after that, I saw an ad for a children's theater company, and I auditioned. I got in the company, and in my second play, I got a lead role. I love singing more than acting, but I like to act because I think it helps with stage presence."

In fact, Taylor had an "amazing stage presence" and "great poise," according to Sharon P. Luyben, the K-12 Music Department Chair of the Wyomissing Area School District. Sharon was Taylor's music teacher at school and was musical director for *The Sound of Music*.

"She was very focused and determined to do what she wanted to do," Sharon said of the young Taylor Swift. "But she was not obnoxiously competitive; not pushy. Just a quiet leader, a pleasant, wonderful person."

Performing in musicals was great experience for Taylor. "That was my first taste of performing in front of people," said Taylor, who was also member of the school drama club and chorus. But ironically, she found her true calling *after* the curtain closed.

Karaoke

After performances in musicals, Taylor would attend cast parties with the rest of the young performers. These parties nudged Taylor onto a different path than theatre. "What I started realizing was that, even more than the musicals, I looked forward to the cast parties afterward because there was a karaoke machine set up at every party,"

Women Who Rock

■ Taylor was inspired by many of country music's favorite female country artists. Here's what she said about these women who rock:

Shania Twain: "Shania is such an independent person and comes off as someone who is so confident and on top of her game," Taylor told *Flare* magazine. "She can hold the crowd's attention like no other artist I've seen. I can only aspire to be like her."

Faith Hill: Faith has "beauty and grace and old school glamour." The two blondes are good friends, and Faith even stood beside Taylor when other country artists questioned her early success. "I think she worked her tail off," Faith said about Taylor's 2009 CMA Entertainer of the Year Award. "She deserves to win."

The Dixie Chicks: Taylor believes these three women brought a "We don't care what you think" quirkiness to country music. In fact, Taylor's favorite song to sing in karaoke was "Goodbye Earl," a daring tune about a woman who murders her abusive husband with the help of her best friend.

Loretta Lynn: One of Taylor's favorite country songs is Lynn's "Fist City." "She says, 'I'll grab you by the hair on your head, and I'll lift you off the ground. I'm not saying my baby's a saint, cause he ain't,'" Taylor recalled of the song. "Isn't that a cool line?"

Dolly Parton: Taylor appreciates Dolly's sense of humor when dealing with male fans who shout out sweet words during a concert. "Dolly Parton had the best response to that kind of thing," Taylor said. "Some guy screamed from the crowd 'I love you, Dolly!' and she goes, 'I thought I told you to stay in the truck!' I'm going to start saying that."

she explained. "That's when I got to sing country music. I got to sing Dixie Chicks songs and Shania Twain songs and Faith Hill songs."

People began to notice how good Taylor was at singing country music, and the more she sang karaoke, the more she loved it. It became evident to Taylor and her parents that singing country music was the path she should follow. "My singing sounded a lot more country than Broadway," she explained. So Taylor sang karaoke and entered contests everywhere possible, at festivals, fairs and parties.

During the summers, while her family stayed at their summer home in Stone Harbor, New Jersey, Taylor sang karaoke at Henny's Restaurant on Third Avenue. Johnny Petillo, who began hosting the karaoke nights in 1989, was very impressed when he first heard 10-year-old Taylor sing. "I knew right then that nothing was gonna stop this kid," Petillo said of Taylor, who would wait patiently to sing almost any song. "She had that determination. You could see it. You could feel it…She loved to be on the stage. She loved having an audience. And she wasn't one of those spoiled, bratty kids we often get in there for karaoke. She was polite."

Taylor used to beg her parents to take her to Henny's every night for karaoke. "That was one of the first things that tipped my parents off that I was gonna be obnoxious about wanting to [sing]," she noted.

Back in Pennsylvania, Taylor often spent hours looking through the phone book, looking for places to sing. It wasn't long before she discovered a karaoke contest at the Pat Garrett Roadhouse, what Taylor described as "a broken-down roadhouse" in Strausstown, Pennsylvania. The owner of the roadhouse hosted performances by traditional country artists—like George Jones, Loretta Lynn, and Charlie Daniels—at his amphitheater across the street.

"If you won the karaoke contest, you got to open up for them," Taylor said of the contest. "You got to play at like 10:00 AM when George Jones would go on at like 8:00 PM. I would go there every single week until I won, and I got the chance to open up for Charlie Daniels. That was something that was just really exciting to me when I was like 11."

It actually took Taylor a year and a half of performing every week to win that contest, just another amazing way she showed her commitment to doing what she loved. By that point, she knew that music had a hold on her like nothing else. "Music was always subliminally

the thing that drew my attention," she said. "I started to realize it when music became all I wanted to think about and all I wanted to do was sing."

Taylor was so dedicated to her music, she sold her horse. Although Taylor enjoyed riding horses, something her mom also did as a child, it was keeping her from what she really loved, which was playing music. Thus, Taylor, who described herself as "driven," sold her horse so she could dedicate herself full time to music.

It was also around this time that Taylor began seeing music as a possible career and not just a hobby. Raised by parents with college diplomas and business degrees, Taylor always assumed she'd work in finance, just like her parents. When people asked Taylor, "What do you want to be when you grow up," she used to say "I'm going to be a stockbroker like my dad." Even though she didn't know what a stockbroker actually did, she wanted to be just like her father. "It wasn't until a few years later that I realized maybe it would be possible to have a career in the thing that I loved, which was music," Taylor said in a *CMT Insider Interview*.

So how does a girl earn a career in country music? Well, for starters, she goes to Nashville.

Faith Hill and Nashville

At age 10, Taylor saw a television program about the life of Faith Hill that truly impacted her life. From that program, Taylor learned that Faith—the wife of Tim McGraw known for hits like "This Kiss" and "Breathe"—decided to go to Nashville to try to make it big. "That's the moment I realized that Nashville is where you need to be if you want to sing country music," Taylor told *The New York Times Style Magazine*. "From that point on, I thought about nothing but getting to Nashville and dreamed about it and imagined in my head what it looked like and how it would be when you finally got there."

Every day, Taylor begged her parents to take her to Nashville. "I was obsessively, obnoxiously bugging my parents every day—'We've got to go to Nashville. Can we go to Nashville? Can we go on a trip to Nashville like now? Or maybe spring break, can we go to Nashville?'" Taylor recalled. "Everything led to that. It was like, 'So how was your day at school today, Taylor?' 'Great. Can we go to Nashville?'"

Her parents finally said yes and one spring break, Taylor, her mom, and her brother drove up and down

Oh Say, Can You See?

■ The national anthem is sung at almost every sports event, big or small. And according to Taylor, it's the perfect song for an aspiring musician to sing. "It's a great way to get in front of a large group of people if you didn't have a record deal," she noted.

Although she enjoyed singing karaoke, Taylor began singing *The Star-Spangled Banner* as a way to get noticed. "I started singing the national anthem anywhere I possibly could, 76ers games, the US Open, and I would just send my tapes out everywhere," explained Taylor. "I would sing the national anthem at garden club meetings. I didn't care. I figured out that if you could sing that one song, you could get in front of 20,000 people without even having a record deal."

Taylor's mom once explained the challenge of singing the national anthem. "The first note to her is critical," Andrea Swift told the *Press of Atlantic City*. "It is one of the hardest songs to perform. If you start out with too low a note, you can't do the end of the song. If you start out too high, it' s the same thing. But Taylor always performs it perfectly."

In 2008 Taylor sang the national anthem for Game 3 of the World Series, which the Philadelphia Phillies ended up winning. At this point in her career, it was an easy song to sing, note-wise. "For me, the national anthem is not as challenging range-wise, because I've been doing it for so long," Taylor said. "The challenge for me is the utter silence that comes over 40,000 people in a baseball stadium and you're the only one singing it. Even though I've sung it hundreds of times, it still gets you a little bit that you're the only one singing and all those people are just focused on the song that you're singing. It's a really surreal moment for me."

Taylor likes to play guitar while singing the National Anthem, which helps make it more of a song and less of a competition. She admitted she still gets the jitters when she sings it, though. "When I get to the high notes at the end, 'And in the rockets' red glare,' I know I'm fine," she said. "From that point out it's free sailing, but it's all about not letting my nerves kick in."

Nashville's Music Row. Her mom would pull the car up to a label, and Taylor would hop out and run inside to give her pitch: "Hey, I'm 11, and I want a record deal. Call me.'"

Taylor admitted she was naïve in thinking she would land a record deal so quickly and at such a young age. "I thought that they might be like, 'Oh, cool, you want a record deal? Here you go. Sign right there,'" she remembered. "I don't think I knew what was going to happen. I knew what would happen if I didn't try, and I knew I would end up staying in the same place and never knowing what would have happened if I hadn't tried."

Taylor is certain that, most of the time, her demo tapes went directly into the wastebasket, even if the receptionist smiled and said, "Oh sure, sweetie. I'll give this to them." But overall, everyone was nice to Taylor and no one ever told her "no."

One strike against Taylor was her age. She was young, and country music did not have a young demographic. Everywhere she went, Taylor was told that only 35-year-old females listen to country music. Taylor knew that wasn't a fact. If she listened to country music, she hypothesized, so did other young girls. "So I kept trying because I didn't believe that there was just one tiny demographic, that there was this one pinpoint you had to hit to be able to apply to country music," she said. "I thought that it could be broader than that."

After spring break, Taylor returned to Pennsylvania without a record deal. But she went home with a huge life lesson. She realized Nashville was full of aspiring singers and songwriters. "It was really more of me looking around this huge town and this huge place that is Nashville and realizing that there were hundreds of thousands of other people that wanted to do exactly what I wanted to do," she said. "I realized that there needed to be something about me that was different, and I needed to figure out something more than I had already figured out. I had figured out the whole performing and singing thing. I just realized I needed something else. So I went back to Pennsylvania and started writing songs and playing guitar."

Writing her own songs was what Taylor believed would set her apart from other young, pretty girls who could sing. "I figured, if I could walk into a room and play my own guitar and sing songs that I've written, they can't touch that," she said. "I can literally not depend on anyone, creatively. That's exactly what I did."

Playing the Twelve-String

Once Taylor picked up a guitar, there was no holding her back. Instead of playing the usual six-string guitar, she chose to play twelve-string guitar, which offers a richer sound. She actually chose twelve-string because someone told her that her fingers were too small to play it. "Anytime someone tells me that I can't do something, I want to do it more," Taylor explained to *Teen Vogue*.

For Taylor, songwriting naturally followed guitar playing. "As soon as I picked up a guitar and learned three chords, I started writing songs," she explained. "Songwriting just came as another form of expression."

Taylor believed that "practice makes perfect," so she played guitar for four hours every day and she wouldn't stop until her mom said it was time for dinner. Often, she played hard enough to make her fingers bleed, and her mom would have to tape them up. This may be one of the reasons Andrea Swift called her daughter an "artistic overachiever."

Playing live music offered Taylor a different feel than singing karaoke, which is sung to prerecorded background music. With a guitar, she felt free to play at more locations. "Instead of playing at karaoke bars and things like that where I needed to drag my little karaoke machine everywhere, I would go with my guitar and I would plug it in at coffee houses," explained Taylor. "And I would bring my little amplifier and plug it in at Boy Scout meetings. I would plug it in at all these different places, little random places where you could play. I now had a portable instrument, and I could go accompany myself, and I could play anywhere I wanted to."

While staying at her family's summer home on the Jersey Shore, Taylor used to sing with her acoustic guitar at a café called Coffee Talk, where she collected tips in a jar. "I used to play for hours and hours in cafes like that," she said, according to *The Philadelphia Inquirer*. "When I would run out of material, I'd just start making up songs on the spot."

This allowed Taylor to improve her guitar playing skills in a very short amount of time. Her songwriting skills also improved. Once every two months, she would take trips to Nashville to play at open mic nights or collaborate with other songwriters. According to *The Envelope (Los Angeles Times)*, it was during one of these trips to Nashville that Taylor first caught the attention of record executive Scott Borchetta, who worked

Poetry and Song Lyrics: Are they the same thing?

■ If you've ever read the lyrics to a song, chances are you noticed the words are formatted the same as a poem. That's because song lyrics are basically poetry set to music. A poem is made up of stanzas, and in song lyrics, these stanzas make up the verses, chorus and bridge of the song. "I've always loved the structure of a song: verse, chorus, verse, chorus, bridge, chorus, then maybe you repeat the first verse," explained Taylor. "I've always operated in those terms and never had to think too much about it, but I've always known it was there."

Some of Taylor's songs start out as poems. Other songs begin with just a title. "It will come into my head, and I'll work backwards from that and I'll get a hook," explained Taylor. Sometimes, Taylor just messes around with her guitar. "A really cool melody will just kind of come at me," she noted. "And which ever way I feel that it goes, either happy or sad, angry or whatever I feel, plays into it. I'll write around that."

Emotion is at the heart of most poetry, and the same is true with Taylor's song lyrics. "It all starts with feeling something," she said. "I think in terms of metaphors a lot of the time… I'll be inspired by something and turn it into a picture that I can see in my head, and then I describe that picture."

for DreamWorks Nashville at the time. Impressed by Taylor's precocious self-confidence and her demo tapes, Scott requested Taylor's father keep in contact with him about Taylor's progress. The two men kept in touch in the following years as Taylor's music continued to evolve.

Taylor's first songs were very basic. Her first song titled "Lucky You" was made up of only three chords—because she knew only three chords then. "It's a G and a D and a C, then back to D," Taylor recalled of her first song. "The song was about a girl who didn't fit in and she didn't care and she was different than everyone else. I think there's a long chorus of me singing 'Do do do do do do do do do do.'"

In fact, versions of this song found their way onto the internet. "You can hear my chipmunk 12-year-old voice singing that song," said Taylor, who was at first a bit dismayed when she realized people had posted the song online. "It's very young and I look back, and it's kind of interesting to hear those kind of storylines and the lyrics that I used to write compared to the lyrics that I write now."

In addition to writing her own music, Taylor also enjoyed singing the national anthem at sports events. She worked her way up from performing at small, local events to national ones. In August 2002, when she sang at the U.S. Open Tennis Tournament in New York, she captured the attention of a young music and entertainment manager named Dan Dymtrow, who also rep-

resented Britney Spears. "She blew me away with her talent, creativity, songwriting and personality," Dan said of Taylor, according to the *Press of Atlantic City*.

Working with Dan for several years as her "overall manager," Taylor was able to take her music from local coffee shop to compact disc and beyond.

The Outside

Writing and singing country music did not help Taylor win the popularity contest at school. In fact, it made her an outsider. Unlike Nashville, where country music is the norm, Wyomissing was not a place for a budding country music singer to flourish. "I grew up in Pennsylvania, and growing up in Pennsylvania and wanting to pursue country music, those are two different things," she explained.

Being different caused many social problems for Taylor. Fellow students would make fun of her and even swear at her, saying things like, "Oh, go sing that country [bleep]." Looking back, Taylor understands why she was made to feel like an outcast. She was doing something different, and people are often afraid of what they don't know or understand. Her classmates were already getting into drugs, alcohol, and parties, and Taylor wasn't interested in that. "In school, it really wasn't a socially accepted thing to be off playing at festivals and fairs and singing national anthems on the weekends instead of going to the parties," she said.

Because of her guitar playing and country music, her friends started to distance themselves from her to the point that they would leave the cafeteria lunch table once she took a seat there. It was a difficult time for Taylor, and she tried to find ways to fit in. "I tried to be good at so many things when I was younger," she told *InStyle.* That included trying to play two sports, soccer and basketball. She wasn't good at either of these, although she did play volleyball. She also tried to fit in physically by straightening her naturally curly hair because the girls at school made fun of it and called it "frizzy."

Because she didn't feel like part of a group, Taylor spent a lot of time observing people from afar. Watching people inspired many songwriting ideas. "I would sit on the edge of class and watch people interact with each other," she said. "I'd watch guys flirt with cool girls, and I would watch best friends talk, and I would go home and write about it."

Feeling like an outsider could have had a negative effect on Taylor. It isn't easy to feel good about being different. Sometimes, she even felt like a spy. "I would go to school during the day, and then, after school, I had this life that was completely different," she said. Although she could have turned this into a reason to drink, smoke, or take drugs, she didn't. Taylor knew her attitude was important to her future. She decided to feel good about being an outsider. "It just dawned on me that I had to love being different or else I was going to end up being dark and

angry and frustrated by school," she said.

"You can choose to let it drag you down, or you can find ways to rise above it," she added. "I came to the conclusion that even though people hadn't always been there for me, music had."

Taylor's negative junior high experiences actually helped her write her first published song. One rainy night in January 2004, Taylor was sitting alone in her bedroom and wrote a song in 30 minutes. It was called "The Outside," and it was about feeling like an outcast at school. "I wrote exactly what I was feeling," Taylor said of the honest lyrics.

Thanks to Dan Dymtrow, "The Outside" was selected to appear on a 2004 compilation CD put out by Maybelline called *Chicks with Attitude,* an ongoing project that helps young female artists just starting out in the music business. Dan had recommended the song to Maybelline executives, and they accepted it for the CD, which served as a free gift with a Maybelline products purchase. The CD corresponded with the Chicks with Attitude 2004 Concert Tour, which featured Liz Phair and the Cardigans.

When Taylor found out that her song was being included on the CD, she was actually eating at Taco Bell. "I was ecstatic! I started screaming," she recalled of hearing the good news. "Everybody looked at me like I was crazy."

Later that year, Taylor was also selected by Abercrombie & Fitch as one of 27 "rising stars" for an ad campaign. A black and white photo of Taylor, guitar in hand, not only appeared in the August 2004 issue of *Vanity Fair* magazine, but also inside the Abercrombie & Fitch catalog.

Looking back, Taylor realized her experiences in junior high not only fueled her songwriting and early successes but also taught her a valuable lesson, one she took with her into high school and adulthood. Being different is okay. "When you step out into the real world, you realize that the only place where it's cool to be the same as everyone else is junior high," she said.

And being different can sometimes be a blessing in disguise. It was this pain of feeling left out that brought her closer to her guitar, closer to her music, closer to her songwriting. "It's strange to think how different my life would be right now if I had been one of the cool kids," Taylor noted.

The Big Move

Despite the pain of being an outcast at school, things were looking up for Taylor Swift professionally. At age 13, thanks to regular trips to Nashville and performances there, she signed a development contract with RCA Records in September 2003. Although it wasn't exactly the record deal she'd hoped for, it was a step forward with a major record label. "A development deal is where they're giving you recording time and money to record, but not promising that they'll put an album out," Taylor told *Entertainment Weekly*. "And they can kind of shelve you, in some circumstances."

When she wasn't in Nashville, Taylor was back home in Wyomissing playing guitar and writing songs. But she always kept the lines of communication open with publishers and labels in the country music capital. She would regularly touch base with these record executives and by being persistent, she landed a dream job by age 14. Sony/ATV Music Publishing asked her to come on board as their youngest songwriter to date.

This job offer was great, but it had its consequences. Traveling to Nashville once every few months would no longer be enough for Taylor. She needed to be in Nashville year round to launch her career in songwriting and country music. But that would mean her entire family would have to relocate. Would they do it? Absolutely. Taylor's parents believed in her abilities and decided to move to Nashville to try and make her dream a reality. They moved to Hendersonville in 2004 and Scott Swift traveled for work between the two states for some time to make the transition. According to Taylor's mom, the move was not about Taylor being famous one day; it was about living in a place that offered the things Taylor needed to reach her goal. Country music thrives in Nashville, and its full of singers and songwriters Taylor could be inspired by and learn from.

Songwriting was not only what Taylor loved, but also what made her unique, and she was able to put her songwriting to the test for Sony/ ATV. Working this after school job felt like a "double life;" Taylor would attend Hendersonville High School by day and afterwards, head to downtown Nashville for songwriting sessions. She took her job very seriously, and came into work each day with five to 10 song ideas. Because she worked with veteran songwriters, people who were much older than her, she always tried to be very professional and mature at work.

Moving to Nashville and being a songwriter for Sony/ATV was not an instant recipe for success. Taylor still had to work hard and make difficult decisions after moving to the country music capital. It was a confusing time because she didn't know what the future held. In fact, her development deal with RCA Records was going nowhere. They wanted to keep her in development even longer, without promise of an eventual record deal. It was then that Taylor made a very bold move: she walked away from RCA Records. "It's not a really popular thing to do in Nashville, to walk away from a major record deal," Taylor said of the decision. "But that's what I did, because I wanted to find some place that would

Take it from **Taylor**

■ Many fans write to Taylor asking for advice on how to make it in the music industry. They are aspiring singers and songwriters who value her opinion. Below are Taylor's words of wisdom and tips for launching a successful career in country music.

Remember that nobody makes it the same way. "There are hundreds of country artists and I can pretty much vouch for the fact that nobody 'makes it' the same way. It's always different."

Work your way up. "The way that I made it was that I was a songwriter first. I moved to Nashville and got a publishing deal with Sony, so I was a paid songwriter before I was a singer with a record deal."

Be yourself. "Just figure out who you are as an artist and what you bring. If you sound just like another artist, that's not what you are looking for. You need to sound exactly like you."

Be unique. "Are you one of those guys who wears a cowboy hat on stage, are you one of those guys who plays guitar?; What do you do that makes you different? What's your thing?"

Get noticed. "My advice to you is that you play anywhere you possibly can."

Go to Nashville. "When you come to Nashville—which is pretty much what you have to do, by the way—what do you have to offer?

really put a lot of time and care into this.… I did not want to be on a record label that wanted me to cut other people's stuff. That wasn't where I wanted to be."

The Bluebird Café

While Taylor was writing songs for Sony/ATV, she performed at various arenas in Nashville. She was even featured in a BMI Songwriter's Circle showcase, which took place at the Bitter End nightclub in Greenwich Village, New York City.

Another night, she sang at a new artist showcase at the Bluebird Café, and it was one of those times when she was in the right place at the right time. Out in the audience was Scott Borchetta, who remembered Taylor from her earlier trips to Nashville. By this time, Dreamworks Nashville had gone under, and Scott was launching his own music label and looking for new talent.

"I remember sitting there just kind of…just…is this gonna hit me? And it absolutely did," Scott Borchetta said, recalling that moment in the Bluebird Café when he listened to Taylor sing with his eyes closed. "And so I went and met with the family after that."

Scott wanted to sign Taylor to his label. After walking away from RCA Records, Taylor knew she wanted a smaller, independent label that could give her the attention she needed as well as the freedom to write her own songs. But she would be taking a chance on Scott Borchetta's label, one he hadn't even named yet. "He didn't have a building for it. And he didn't have a staff for it. But he had a dream, and would I go on board?" Taylor recalled to *Dateline NBC*. "I went with my gut instinct which, which just said, 'Say yes.'"

Working with Scott Borchetta, who eventually named his label Big Machine Records, Taylor was able to not only write her own songs but perform them too. She continued to follow the first rule about writing, which is, "Write what you know." Taylor wrote songs about the things she knew a lot about, like boys, crushes, teenage life, and the pressure to fit in. Taylor held nothing back when writing her first songs; she based them so much on her life, she even wrote the names of real boys—like Drew and Cory—in her lyrics, something she continues to do today.

"The funny thing about me is that I kind of say everything that comes to mind and don't really hold too much back," Taylor told *Unrated Magazine*. "I don't have a lot of secrets. Drew and Cory are real people. That's

like a huge question that I get all the time: 'Are they real people?' Yeah, they are people."

Because Taylor wrote about the ups and down of youth, Scott Borchetta also took a chance on Taylor. She was young, and the country music industry still believed that only middle age people listened to country music. It seemed unlikely that Taylor's songs about high school crushes were going to appeal to middle-aged listeners. Still, Taylor stayed true to who she was. She never tried to write about things she hadn't experienced, like marriage or children.

"I'll be the first to stand up and say 'Look, I'm 17! I've never been married or had a kid," Taylor said when she was just starting out. "I can't relate as much to the songs that are about that, as I can to songs that are about things that I have gone through. I think that's why so many young people listen to pop music—because younger people in pop music sing about younger things."

When it came to making it in the music industry, Taylor had a secret weapon that had nothing to do with talent or demographics. Simply put, she believed in herself. "There were times when I didn't know if I was going to get a record deal," she said of the days before she met Scott Borchetta. "But never once did I ever think, I should just give this up, this is just not gonna work.'"

Fortunately, Taylor was also surrounded by positive people. "No one ever said to me, 'Girl, you cannot do this,'" Taylor recalled. "I thank God for that." Her parents also believed in her. "My parents were just so positive and I was able to get through and break through," she said.

Taylor said it was her parents who "empowered" her to do what she loved no matter what. Looking back, she realizes the important role parents have on their children. "There are really two ways to look at it when you are raising kids," she said. "You can either say 'You can be whatever you want to be' and then there is actually believing it. My parents actually believed it."

Because she believed in herself, Taylor followed her instincts. She signed a contract with an unknown label. She wrote songs about high school. And she continued to play country music. And it seems, contrary to popular belief, there were plenty of young country music fans out there ready to hear Taylor's tunes. With her first single "Tim McGraw" and her first album, *Taylor Swift*, she was able to pull not only young country music fans, but middle-aged ones too. She attracted not only country music fans, but pop music fans as well.

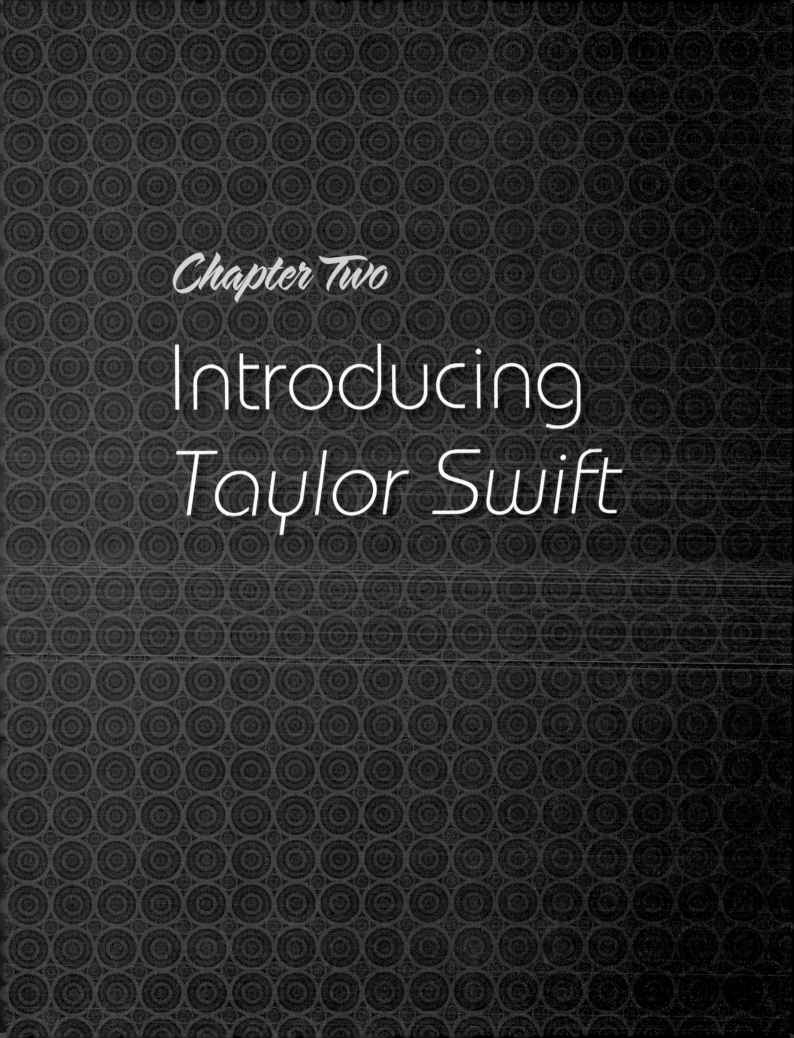

Chapter Two
Introducing Taylor Swift

Even though Taylor first worked as a songwriter for Sony/ATV, her songwriting skills were relatively unknown to the outside world until Big Machine Records released her debut album in October 2006. "I sat down with my record label and went through songs before we started recording," Taylor said about the process of compiling her first album. "There were about 40 that we wanted to put on the CD. But we had to narrow it down."

The result, Taylor's self-titled album, included 11 original songs, all written or co-written by Taylor. This fact immediately separated the 16-year-old from other music stars of her day. They may have had beautiful singing voices but most of them did not write their own music or even play an instrument. Her many talents also helped Taylor make music history. After her self-titled album earned the No. 1 spot on the Country Albums chart and climbed to No. 5 on the Billboard 200 chart, it went platinum, selling one million copies by June 2008. This meant Taylor Swift was the first female solo country artist in history to write or co-write every song on a platinum album.

Going platinum was a huge accomplishment for Taylor, but it proved to be just the beginning of her success. In November 2009, with over four million copies sold, Taylor's self-titled album became the longest-charting album of the decade, a spot previously held by Nickelback, a rock band Taylor likes. "That's a crazy statistic," Taylor noted to *MTV News*. "It means that my first album that came out, the self-titled album, has been on the charts longer than I guess any album this century."

Why was her first album so successful? According to Taylor, it's because of her fans, whom she thanks at every music milestone. "When things like that happen, I love the fans more and more," she said. "And I didn't think I could love them any more for all the things they've done for me, especially in the last year."

Taylor's fans are a huge part of the equation because they are the ones who buy her music in stores and online. But another reason for Taylor's success is her songwriting. She has won over fans young and old with honest lyrics, thought-provoking topics, and catchy melodies. Most of Taylor's songs are based on her real-life experiences or the experiences of people she knows. Sometimes, they are based simply on feelings she has had or imagined. In this way, Taylor reveals her inner self through her music. "If you listen to my albums, it's like reading my diary," she told *The New York Times Style Magazine*.

Like any teenage girl's diary, Taylor's debut album is full of stories about love, something she's always been fascinated with. "I am a complete hopeless romantic," she told *CMT News*. The songs encompass a wide range of topics on love—from first loves to break ups, from unrequited love to relationships that stand the test of time. "There is no strategy or rulebook when it comes to love," she explained to *Flare*. "No amount of advice can prepare you for its ups and downs. It's unpredictable; that's why I write about it."

Teenage girls think about more than just crushes and boys, though; they're also concerned with body image and the pressures of fitting in, and Taylor's first album explores these important issues as well. No matter the tune—whether it's her first single "Tim McGraw" or her pop crossover hit "Teardrops on My Guitar"—every song on the self-titled album tells a story, and every story is told with honesty and creativity, which seem to be the trademarks of this gifted songwriter.

"Tim McGraw"

When it comes to writing about personal experience, Taylor's first single, "Tim McGraw" is a perfect example. According to *Blender* magazine, Taylor wrote the song after a relationship with a boy named Drew—a hockey player who was three years older than Taylor—ended. The two broke up when Drew went off to college, leaving Taylor back at home missing him. When she thought back about the year she spent with Drew—whether it was taking prom pictures in his backyard or her first kiss—one of the things she realized she would miss the most was listening to Tim McGraw songs, specifically the tune "Can't Tell Me Nothin'"

"All of my friends know that my favorite songs are Tim McGraw songs," said Taylor, who wrote the song in only 15 minutes during high school math class. "It's a song about two people who fall in love and are brought together by country music. And even when they're apart, every time they hear that song, it takes them right back to that place. For me, the song is about the haunting power of country music."

At first, Taylor did not think the song would be a hit. "I kind of shelved it for like three months and never even thought it was going to be a single," said Taylor. "But my label heard it, and was like 'We're putting that out.'"

Taylor's first single, "Tim McGraw," was about her first boyfriend. She later became friends with the song's namesake, country singer Tim McGraw and his wife, Faith Hill.

"What Drew Says"

■ Working relationship details into song lyrics is a daring move; it comes with consequences because the boys Taylor writes about eventually hear the songs they inspired. So what do Taylor's ex-crushes and ex-boyfriends think of her songs?

"Sometimes they won't really contact me, but they'll put it on their MySpace page," Taylor explained to *Life Story*. "You know, 'By the way, Taylor Swift wrote a song about me. E-mail me if you want to know more'—just really annoying things like that where they get a big head all of a sudden."

Taylor's ex-boyfriend Drew, who inspired "Tim McGraw" and "Our Song," actually bought her self-titled album and liked it. "He really thought it was cool that, [even though] we weren't going out anymore, I remembered our relationship nicely," Taylor noted. "I think that he was happy that I didn't write 'Picture To

Burn' about him."

Taylor said she and her first boyfriend don't talk that often because "his new girlfriend isn't too much of a fan." But she admitted it's generally hard to stay friends with an ex-boyfriend, unless you're trying to get back together with him. "I don't know if you can ever truly go back to the place it was before you dated," she said. "I just don't know what to say to that person any more, like, 'How are you and how's your new girlfriend? Awesome! Good to talk to you.'"

Taylor's first boyfriend was not only the inspiration for the song "Tim McGraw," but also for a casting decision in the video. An actor named Clayton Collins played Taylor's love interest in the video. "The guy that 'Tim McGraw' was written about looked a lot like the guy we picked for the video," she said. "That was done on purpose. He was really tall with dark hair."

In fact, Taylor's father, Scott Swift, suggested she play the song for Big Machine Records president Scott Borchetta, who loved it so much, he immediately proclaimed it would be her first single. "That was the moment of 'Oh my God,'" Scott said of hearing "Tim McGraw" the first time. "And the grenade dropped in the still pond."

The song was originally called "When You Think Tim McGraw" but over time, the title was shortened to simply "Tim McGraw." Taylor wrote the original version but tweaked some of the notes and lyrics at the piano with her songwriting partner, Liz Rose.

Big Machine Records released "Tim McGraw" in June 2006, a few months before the complete album was released. The tune peaked at No. 6 on the Billboard Country Songs chart and at No. 40 on the Billboard Hot 100 chart. It was an immediate hit with country music fans because it specifically mentioned the hunky country superstar Tim McGraw, best known for the songs "Something Like That," "I Like it, I Love it" and "Live Like You Were Dying," to name a few. In creative writing, this is called an allusion, a reference to a person, place, thing or phrase. In the lyrics, Taylor alludes to Tim McGraw, assuming the listener knows who he is and is familiar with his music. This was an especially smart songwriting decision on Taylor's part because most country music fans already had their own feelings and memories about Tim McGraw's music, and this helped them immediately connect with her song. In the lyrics, Taylor also mentions specific details about life in the country, like "Georgia stars," "Chevy truck," and "back roads," that help paint a picture of the song's setting.

Even fans of other music genres like pop and rock appreciate the lyrics of "Tim McGraw" because the song is ultimately about the powerful connection between music and memory. Like our sense of smell, music can bring about nostalgia, a longing for the past. Because songs usually represent the time period in which they are recorded, music helps people remember moments from the past, like a first kiss. "I think the reason why 'Tim McGraw' worked out was, it was reminiscent, and it was thinking about a relationship that you had and then lost," Taylor told *Entertainment Weekly*. "I think one of the most powerful human emotions is what should have been and wasn't. I think everyone can relate to that. That was a really good first song to start out on, just because a lot of people can relate to wanting what you can't have."

Taylor and her fiddler, Caitlin Evanson, work well together. Many of Taylor's songs rely on fiddle to create country charm.

Taylor took a big risk by putting Tim McGraw's name in her song, though. She had never met him before, and it was only a matter of time before Tim—the son of the late Tug McGraw, who pitched for both the New York Mets and the Philadelphia Phillies—heard the song. "I've heard from people that he and Faith [Hill] love the song, which was awesome to hear," Taylor said.

In May 2007, almost a year after the song was released, Taylor finally met Tim McGraw and his wife, country singer Faith Hill, in person at the Academy of Country Music Awards. "He was so nice, and Faith was absolutely amazing," she later told *Florida Entertainment Scene*. "We were talking about how excited we were to be going on tour together."

Later that year, in November 2007, Taylor proudly took home a BMI Country Award for co-writing the song "Tim McGraw."

"Picture to Burn"

Unlike the song "Tim McGraw," which describes the positive side of an ended relationship, Taylor's song

"Picture to Burn," the second track on her self-titled album, is all about the negative part. It's about a "redneck" guy who did a girl wrong. "I didn't get my perfect fantasy/I realize you love yourself more than you could love me," Taylor states in the song, which she once again co-wrote with Liz Rose.

Though she's never disclosed the name of the boy who inspired the song, she did say this about him: "The guy I wrote this song about, I didn't really ever 'officially' date. We almost dated. It really bothered me that he was so cocky and that is where that song came from."

Taylor wrote "Picture to Burn" one day after school, something she usually did because her job after school was writing songs for Sony/ATV in downtown Nashville.

"I found myself just sitting there with my guitar going, 'I hate his stupid truck that he doesn't let me drive. He's such a redneck! Oh my God!'" Taylor explained. "That actually became the chorus to the song, so that's one of the most honest songs I've ever written."

The song lyrics are feisty and aggressive. In "Picture to Burn," Taylor threatens to do a few things in revenge, like date the jerky ex-boyfriend's best friends and in one version, even tell her friends he's gay. With lyrics like "wasted time" and "planning my revenge," Taylor shows a different side. She may be sweet and nice, but if you cross her, look out. She'll strike a match and not only burn your picture, but your memory.

Taylor's fans, mostly women, relate to these heartbreak songs as much as they do her romantic ones. They appreciate Taylor's honesty, that she's willing to discuss the bad times as well as the good. To Taylor, it's important to debunk the myths about love. "We're raised as little girls to think that we're a princess and that Prince Charming is going to sweep us off our feet. And that we're going to ride off into the sunset on a white horse," Taylor told *CMT News*. "We're not really expecting to get blown off or ignored or broken up with or cheated on.… I think it's really interesting when you come to terms with that reality: 'Maybe that's not gonna happen with this guy because this guy's a jerk.'"

"Picture to Burn" speaks to so many fans because it's about an act of revenge and destruction. Just like Carrie Underwood's hit song "Before He Cheats," about a girl who destroys her boyfriend's truck because he's been untrue to her, "Picture to Burn" suggests setting fire to old photographs or letters, destroying any evidence of the relationship. In fact, Taylor further explored this theme in her video for the song. The video co-stars her band and her best friend, Abigail Anderson, who helped trash the video boyfriend's place using toilet paper.

"Teardrops on My Guitar"

While a student at Hendersonville High School, Taylor fell hard for another boy named Drew with "beautiful eyes" and an "amazing smile." She sat next to him in class and admitted to having a big crush on him.

"I was definitely in the 'friend zone,'" Taylor explained while serving as Artist of the Month on the *Great American Country* (GAC) blog. "He would talk to me every day about his girlfriend, and how happy they were, and how awesome she was and blah, blah, blah. I would just sit there and fake a smile and tell him how happy I was for him. I never told him that I liked him, and it absolutely was killing me. So I wrote a song with his name in it, and this song is definitely the product of that — never being able to tell them that you like them."

Taylor came up with the idea for "Teardrops on My Guitar" on her way home from school one day. "I was just like 'Oh my God; I got this idea in my head," she remembered thinking. The song is about a girl in love with a boy unaware of her feelings: "Drew looks at me/I fake a smile so he won't see/What I want and what I need/And everything that we should be."

Writing "Teardrops on My Guitar" actually helped Taylor work through her crush on Drew. "I think a lot of people have been through that, where it is just killing you. You want to be able to tell them, but you can't," she said. "I came to the realization that, if I am his friend, I'll do anything to make him happy—even if what makes him happy isn't me. That was kind of a hard thing to come to terms with, and one way was to write this song."

Falling in love with a friend is a popular theme not only in music, but in literature and films. But Taylor and her collaborator, Liz Rose, made her song different by playing with words. It's common to say teardrops fall onto cheeks on even onto a pillow, but having the teardrops fall onto a guitar added another dimension to the song. For one, it portrayed the girl in the song as a musician, which connected Taylor to the tune, since she plays and writes songs on her guitar. It also paints a sad picture of a girl crying while strumming an instrument. She pours out her feelings into her music, sort of like singing the blues.

Taylor and Liz also used repetition to bring about meaning. The line "the only thing that keeps me wishing on a wishing star" is unique in that it could have been written as "wishing on a falling star" or "wishing on a shooting star." Instead, they chose to repeat the word "wishing," which further demonstrates the girl's desire, the hope she will someday tell the boy how she feels and that perhaps, he'll feel the same.

As a musician, Taylor made other decisions unrelated to the lyrics that helped make "Teardrops on My Guitar" a success. The original version on her self-titled album sounds much more like country music than pop because it's missing a background beat most common in pop music. To help the song crossover into the pop genre, Taylor said she made a "no-brainer" decision to add that background beat. It was a smart decision because the new pop version of "Teardrops on My Guitar" peaked at No. 13 on the Billboard Hot 100 and later peaked at No. 5 on the Mediabase Top 40 and Billboard Adult Contemporary chart. The song was later named "Country Song of the Year" at the BMI Country Awards in November 2007.

Two years after the song came out, Taylor's crush named Drew finally took the hint from the song "Teardrops on My Guitar" and showed up at Taylor's house unexpectedly. "I was on my way out of the house to meet Carrie [Underwood] and Kellie [Pickler] for a hockey game," Taylor said. "He was standing there in my driveway. I haven't talked to this guy in two years. I was like, 'Um, hi?'"

Taylor said it would have been "cool" and "poetic" had Drew showed up at her house right after the song was released. But as time went by, her life and her feelings for him had changed. "He just randomly decided to show up in my driveway and I was like 'You're late. What's the deal?'" she said.

After that night, Drew continued to phone Taylor a few times but she never returned his calls. "I've actually gotten a few missed calls from Mr. 'Teardrops On My Guitar.' I'm not going back, because he's still got a girlfriend," she told *Unrated Magazine*. "What am I gonna say? That's probably the number one most awkward conversation ever."

In the end, Taylor feels like she won. Drew may not have liked her back in the day, but she went on to find success despite the unrealized relationship. "You know you don't get the guy, but you get a song that goes to radio and does well for you and makes you smile," she said. "So it kind of works out to your advantage no matter what happens."

"A Place in This World"

Taylor's fourth track on her self-titled album, "A Place in This World," was inspired not by an ex-boyfriend or crush, but her own journey to becoming a singer/songwriter. "I wrote this song when I was 13 and had just moved to Nashville," said Taylor of the song. "It was tough trying to find out how I was going to get where I wanted to go. I knew where I wanted to be, but I just didn't know how to get there."

In this vein, the song is about a girl trying to figure out who she is and where she wants to go in life: "I'm alone, on my own and that's all I know/ I'll be strong, I'll be wrong, oh, but life goes on/ Oh, I'm just a girl trying to find a place in this world."

Like the song suggests, with lines like, "I don't know what's down this road" and "Tomorrow's just a mystery," the future once seemed unclear to Taylor Swift; all she had was a dream. After realizing Pennsylvania was not the place to launch a country music career, Taylor's family moved to be near Nashville, home of the Grand Ole Opry and known as the Country Music Capital. They relocated to a Nashville suburb of about 40,000 people called Hendersonville, Tennessee—once the home of the late Johnny Cash and the late Roy Orbison. Taylor's dad commuted back and forth between Tennessee and Pennsylvania, something Taylor called an "incredible sacrifice."

Success did not come immediately to Taylor; she had to work for it and be very patient. "I had people tell me, "Wait. Later. We'll sign you to a record deal later," she explained. Although she eventually landed a development deal with RCA Records, she chose to walk away because the deal never resulted in a record. "I just did not want it to happen with the method of 'Let's throw this up against the wall and see if it sticks, and if it doesn't, we'll just walk away,'" she said. "I wanted a record label that needed me, that absolutely was counting on me to succeed."

It was a scary decision because Taylor had no guarantee whether another music label would be interested in her music. But just like the words of her song "Maybe I'm just a girl on a mission/But I'm ready to fly," she took a risk and based her decision on her instinct.

It was a very vulnerable time for Taylor, something

Playing with
Rhyme

■ Rhyme is a common element of any song, and it's something Taylor loves to play with. "I love rhymes, and I love poetry, and I can't get enough of it," she told *InStyle* magazine. "I love finding words that rhyme and searching through my mind to find the perfect one. It's so much fun!"

Of course, there are different kinds of rhyme, and Taylor seems to try them all. Below are the varying uses of rhyme, and the ways Taylor applies them to her lyrics.

TRUE RHYME is the most common rhyme. It is the first rhyming we learn as kids, when we realize the words "cat" and "hat" and "bat" have the same ending sound. Taylor uses true rhyme in many of her songs:

"Cold As You": "And now that I'm sitting here, thinking it through/I've never been anywhere cold as you."

"Tim McGraw": "He says he's so in love, he's finally got it right/ I wonder if he knows he's all I think about at night."

True rhyme can occur at places other than at the end of a line. Sometimes, it's fun to use true rhyme within a line, which is called INTERNAL RHYME, as Taylor does in the following examples:

The Outside: "I can't see you, this isn't the best view."

"A Place in this World": "I'll be strong, I'll be wrong."

And then there's APPROXIMATE RHYME, also known as near rhyme or oblique rhyme. This is rhyme that is not quite perfect. The two words sound similar, but do not have the exact same ending sound.

"Tim McGraw": "And I was right there beside him all summer long/And then the time we woke up to find that summer gone."

"A Place in This World": "Oh, I'm just a girl/ trying to find a place in this world."

"Should've Said No": "You shouldn't be begging for forgiveness at my feet/You should've said no/Baby and you might still have me."

she refers to in the song with the cliché "wearing my heart on my sleeve." It's a common saying people use to mean that they are revealing who they truly are and opening themselves up to get hurt. After walking away from RCA, Taylor continued to follow her passion, which was writing and performing her own songs. She continued to do shows at open mic nights. And it was while she was doing what she loved that her life changed forever. She met Scott Borchetta, a record executive who was starting his own label called Big Machine Records. Taylor signed with Scott, again making the decision with her "gut instinct."

The rest, as they say, is history. But it's a history and a journey Taylor will never forget. Nor will she take for granted her successes. Within the lyrics of "A Place in This World" is this secret message: "Found it."

"Cold As You"

Like "Picture to Burn," Taylor's fifth song on the self-titled album "Cold as You" is laced with anger and disappointment.

"I think the lyrics to this song are some of the best we've ever written," said Taylor, who co-wrote the song with Liz Rose. "It's about that moment where you realize someone isn't at all who you thought they were, and that you've been trying to make excuses for someone who doesn't deserve them. And that some people are just never going to love you. We were halfway through writing this when I started singing And now that I'm sitting here thinking it through, I've never been anywhere cold as you."

Though Taylor sometime names boys in the lyrics of her songs, she did not mention the particular boy who inspired "Cold as You." She has, however, noted some of the jerky things boys have said and done to her in the past. "I remember when I broke up with a guy, he looked at me and said, 'I can't believe how much money I spent on you,'" she told *Girl's Life*. "That was the worst experience as far as gifts go, because it made me regret every awesome gift he had ever given me. Like 'Wow, I didn't realize you were counting up the dollars in your head.'"

It's likely Taylor based the song "Cold as You" on negative experiences such as this one. Taylor works the arrogant and selfish behavior of some boys into the lyrics with the lines, "When you take, you take the very best of me," "Every smile you fake is so condescending," and "You never did a damn thing, honey." She also illustrates her emotional pain in response to this behavior with lines like "Counting all the scars you made." Scars can refer to physical wounds, like a cut, but they can also represent painful memories and feelings.

The song's biggest triumph, however, is the chorus, which plays on the word "cold," a word with several definitions and uses. A "cold" person is said to be un-emotional and perhaps even mean; on the other hand, when it comes to weather, "cold" is the opposite of hot and brings to mind low temperatures. Taylor bridges these two ideas by saying "I've never been anywhere cold as you." It's a unique line because she's comparing the selfish boy to wintry places she might travel, and it can be assumed he's colder than somewhere known for freezing temperatures, like Alaska.

Writing heartfelt songs about being mistreated by a boy shows a very sensitive side of Taylor, but it's a side she wants to show to her fans. "I really don't think there should be a wall between artists and fans," she said. "That's why my album is so personal. I think it's just better to be honest with people. Being vulnerable isn't always a bad thing, especially when it comes to expression."

"The Outside"

Taylor's song "The Outside" originally appeared on Maybelline's *Chicks with Attitude* compilation CD and later became the sixth track on her self-titled album. Written when she was just 12 years old, the song describes how Taylor felt during middle school and junior high. The lyrics state, "How can I ever try to be better/ Nobody ever lets me in/I can still see you, this ain't the best view/On the outside looking in."

"The Outside" is an accurate title for the song because Taylor felt like an outsider when she was growing up in Wyomissing, Pennsylvania. "I was a lot different than all the other kids, and I never really knew why," Taylor explained. "I was taller, and sang country music at karaoke bars and festivals on weekends while other girls went to sleepovers. Some days, I woke up not knowing if anyone was going to talk to me that day."

One of the reasons Taylor felt like an outcast was that she originally attended the private Wyncroft School in Pottstown, Pennsylvania. When she transferred to the public school in Wyomissing, she was a new student among kids who had gone to school together from an early age. Taylor definitely wasn't part of the cool crowd or popular clique. "You know how there's always that

popular girl? I was never that girl," she told *Life Story*. "I was always a few levels below that. While in middle school and junior high, all my friends ditched me and all of a sudden, I had no friends, I was really lonely."

When Taylor uses the word 'ditch', she means it. Sometimes, her friends would leave the table in the cafeteria after she sat down. Another time, they purposely went shopping at the mall without her. They made fun of her curly and sometimes frizzy hair so much so that Taylor tried straightening her hair just to fit in. The girls at school also disliked her taste in music. Country music was not popular in Pennsylvania.

Just as she did in the song "Tim McGraw," Taylor uses an allusion in the song "The Outside" to bring about meaning. In the tune, she says "I tried to take the road less traveled by," which refers to a poem titled "The Road Not Taken" by American poet Robert Frost. The poem ends with a famous line about two roads: "I took the one less traveled by/And that has made all the difference." By using the words "the road less traveled," Taylor is saying she tried to do things differently than most people her age. Even in junior high, her friends were getting into drugs and alcohol and partying, while she was singing karaoke and performing at open mic nights.

The best part of the song "The Outside" is that many years after Taylor first wrote the song, she discovered a happy ending. At age 12, instead of feeling bad about herself, Taylor used her pain to fuel her passion in life: songwriting. Music became the outlet for her pain and she found a best friend in her guitar. Taylor wasn't one of the cool kids, and so she dedicated her life to music, ultimately becoming a platinum-selling country and pop music sensation (who's pretty cool).

"Tied Together with a Smile"

One of the biggest issues young adults face every day is body image, especially teenage girls. Many girls obsess about their weight. Thin actresses and models set a standard that young girls find impossible to achieve, and this ends up making them feel bad about their bodies. When girls feel so bad about their bodies, they sometimes turn to desperate measures to look thin. Anorexia, the act of starving yourself, or bulimia, the act of overeating and then forcing yourself to vomit, are two prevalent eating disorders among young women, and even some young men.

Rain, Rain, Go Away

■ It seems Taylor Swift is fascinated with the rain. The rain motif—a recurring or repeating theme or pattern—shows up in many of her songs. In fact, the title of one of her songs on her platinum edition *Fearless* album is "Come in with the Rain." She even covered Rihanna's song "Umbrella" on her *Live from Soho* album.

So why does Taylor write about the rain so much? Rain has long been a symbol of sorrow; it makes listeners think of dark, gloomy skies, or, in the worst case, a treacherous storm. It is also used to represent tears. Below are a few of the rain-or water-themed lines from Taylor's self-titled album.

"A Place in this World": "I'm just walking trying to see through the rain coming down."

"Cold As You": "What a rainy ending given to a perfect day."

"Tied Together with a Smile": "The water's high, you're jumping into it."
"But he leaves you out like a penny in the rain."

"Stay Beautiful": "I'm taking pictures so I can save them for a rainy day."

Making **Comparisons**

■ Song lyrics can be more descriptive through the use of similes and metaphors. The two literary devices are similar in concept but different in how they are applied. A simile compares two things using the word "like" or "as." On the other hand, a metaphor compares two things without using "like" or "as." A metaphor usually relies on a state-of-being verb like "is" or "are." Taylor uses both similes and metaphors to make her song lyrics powerful, descriptive, and heartfelt.

Similes

"Tim McGraw": "The moon like a spotlight on the lake."

"Tied Together with a Smile": "'Cause you're giving it away like it's extra change."

"Stay Beautiful": "Cory's eyes are like a jungle."
"He smiles, it's like the radio."

"Mary's Song": "But your eyes still shined like pretty lights."

Metaphors

"Teardrops on My Guitar": "He's the song in the car I keep singing."

"Our Song": "Our Song is the slamming screen door."
"Our song is the way you laugh."

"Stay Beautiful": "If you and I are a story that never gets told."
"If what you are is a daydream that I never get to hold."

Taylor tackled the issue of eating disorders in her song "Tied Together with a Smile," which appears as the seventh track on her self-titled album. The song was inspired by one of Taylor's friends in high school who was bulimic. According to Taylor, the girl was gorgeous. "All the guys want to date her and all the girls want to be her," she explained. "She is literally a pageant queen."

Taylor wrote the song right after she discovered her friend had an eating disorder. "That is one of those moments when your heart kind of stops," she said. "How can somebody who seems so strong have such a horrible, horrible weakness? Something that is killing her."

This beauty pageant winner did not see herself as beautiful. That's evident in the first lines of the song: "Seems the only one who doesn't see your beauty/Is the face in the mirror looking back at you." It was hard for Taylor to believe this girl didn't think of herself as beautiful, but she soon realized things are not always as they seem. "Sometimes when you get a little closer to people who look that perfect, you realize that they don't *feel* perfect," Taylor explained to *Seventeen*. "They feel like they're ugly."

The girl in the song is "tied together with a smile" because although she's falling apart inside, she's smiling on the outside so no one knows her pain. Taylor illustrates this point with the line "You don't tell anyone that you might not be the golden one."

Taylor admitted "Tied Together with a Smile" proved a challenge to write. "I wasn't just telling some sad story," she said. "This was real." And it's real not only for her friend, but also for millions of other young girls. According to the Alliance for Eating Disorders Awareness, 24 million Americans struggle with an eating disorder, and 90 percent of the women with eating disorders are between the ages of 12 and 25. Taylor never meant the song to be a lecture, but she did want to highlight this problem among young women.

"I always thought that one of the biggest overlooked problems American girls face is insecurity," she said. "Whether insecurity spurs anorexia or whether it spurs some other eating disorder, or not liking yourself, or suicide, or hurting other people. It is all based from insecurity, and not being okay with yourself. I think that if people could just be confident about who they are and what they stand for, there would be fewer problems in the world."

It's normal to feel bad about yourself from time to time. Even Taylor questions her looks. Once, when she read a comment online about her eyes being small, she started to worry that her eyes were too small. Although Taylor boasts a very lean figure, she admits food is her weakness. "I don't diet. I don't like it. For me, I would eat healthy, but I refuse to use the term 'diet,'" she said. "For a while there, I put out a single and I was like, 'I gotta get in shape man, I'm going on a diet.' And then I realized that's ridiculous. I'm happy with how I look and I'm not gonna you know...if I want to eat a cheeseburger, it's going to happen."

Although she has a treadmill on her tour bus, she doesn't overdo it when it comes to working out either. "The only time I run is when I'm gearing up for a tour, and I know I need some serious endurance so I'm not going to be panting onstage," she said.

So what happened to Taylor's friend, the one who struggled with bulimia? Taylor played the song "Tied Together with a Smile" for her and it helped.

"Luckily, I talked to her about it, and she got help and she is fine now," said Taylor.

"Stay Beautiful"

Just like "Teardrops on my Guitar," which names a boy named Drew, the song "Stay Beautiful" names a boy named Cory. Was this one of Taylor's boyfriends? Not exactly.

"This is a song I wrote about a guy I never dated," she said. "A guy I

thought was cute, and never really talked to him much. But something about him inspired this song, just watching him."

This is one of Taylor's greatest gifts as a songwriter; her ability to write about things she only imagines. She doesn't need to have a relationship with a boy to write a song about him. "After hearing my songs, a lot of people ask me, 'How many boyfriends have you HAD?'" she said. "And I always tell them that more of my songs come from observation than actual experience."

Taylor said she can look across a crowded room or simply make eye contact with a guy, and it's enough to inspire a song. "It can just be 'I am having a conversation with a guy, he is flirting with me and then his girlfriend walks up,'" she said. "You can write a couple of songs about that. "

"Stay Beautiful" describes a boy named Cory with eyes like a jungle—perhaps meaning they are vividly green like the flora and fauna of a jungle, or perhaps they are wild and exciting. When he smiles, Taylor says

Secret Messages: A Matching Game

■ Inspired by the Beatles—who were said to have encoded secret messages on their records that could only be heard only by playing the songs backward—Taylor encoded secret messages in the lyrics printed inside her CD jacket. Each song includes random capital letters that when written down in the order they appear spell out a unique phrase. Think you know which secret messages go with which songs? Take this matching quiz.

1. Tim McGraw	A. Found It
2. Picture to Burn	B. Time to Let Go
3. Teardrops on My Guitar	C. Sam, Sam, Sam, Sam
4. A Place in This World	D. You are Not Alone
5. Cold as You	E. Date Nice Boys
6. The Outside	F. Live N' Love
7. Tied Together with a Smile	G. Sometimes Love is Forever
8. Stay Beautiful	H. You are Loved
9. Should've Said No	I. Can't Tell Me Nothin'
10. Mary's Song (Oh My My My)	J. He Will Never Know
11. Our Song	K. Shake N Bake

Answers: 1. (J) 2. (E) 3. (J) 4. (A) 5. (B) 6. (D) 7. (H) 8. (K) 9. (C) 10. (G) 11. (F)

it's like the radio, as if he's whispering songs into the girl's window, songs with words that no one else understands. But Cory doesn't know he's special to this girl. She wishes that she'll end up with Cory someday, but if that doesn't happen, she wants him to know he should stay as beautiful as he is today.

This theme of being secretly in love with someone occurs in other songs by Taylor, like "Teardrops on My Guitar." It's a feeling Taylor is familiar with from personal exprience. "I'm the girl who—I call it 'girl-next-door-itis'—the hot guy is friends with, and gets all his relationship advice from, but never considers dating," she admitted to *Teen Vogue*.

What was it about Cory that Taylor liked from afar? What does she find attractive about a particular boy? Sometimes that's actually hard for her to say. "You can't predict who you'll fall in love with," she said. "Love's the one thing that doesn't have a pattern—it's a total mystery. If you overthink it, you're wasting your time."

"Should've Said No"

Being named in a Taylor Swift song is not too bad for your reputation if your name is Drew or Cory, but if

your name is Sam, look out. Taylor wrote the song "Should've Said No" about her ex-boyfriend Sam. "He's the guy who made the unfortunate error of cheating on a songwriter," Taylor told *Blender*. "Big mistake."

Taylor doesn't mention Sam's name in the words of the song, but she spelled his name out several times in a secret message encoded in the CD jacket lyrics.

At one time, Taylor dated Sam, but once she found out he cheated on her with another girl, she broke it off. "There's always that moment where you're like 'He says he's not gonna do it again, he says he's sorry, and oh, look how sorry he is!' But they're not sorry," she told *Seventeen*. "If they cheated on you, then you didn't matter enough for them to be thinking about you while it was happening. So what does it matter if he apologizes after the fact? And at some point, you realize you do not deserve to be treated like that. I decided I didn't want to be *that* girl."

The song, which sort of mimics the "Just Say No" anti-drug campaign of the 1980s, states "You should've said no baby, and you might still have me." Though the song is about cheating on a girlfriend, according to Taylor, it applies to many mistakes we make in life. "Just being a human being, I've realized that before every big problem you create for yourself, before every huge mess you have to clean up, there was a crucial moment where you could've just said no," she said.

It's clear in the song that at one time the relationship was good. It was full of "songs," "flowers," and "smiles." But all of that changes once the girl in the song learns the truth, that her boyfriend cheated on her in what he called "a moment of weakness."

Writing about Sam, also known as "Bad Cheater Guy," was therapeutic for Taylor. It helped her get over her anger and disappointment. "Usually, like after I write a song about somebody, I kind of get over it," she said. "If it's a heartbreak song or something like it, it usually helps me get through it."

In some ways, it was also a form of revenge. Slipping Sam's name into the secret message of the CD jacket was enough to make the real Sam nervous. "It was only his first name, but everyone fig-

ured it out," Taylor divulged to *Women's Health*. "I'd get texts from him. He was scared out of his mind that I'd crucify him on a talk show. All I could think was, 'Well, you *should've* said no.' That's what the song is about."

Now, Taylor is a lot smarter about where, and with whom, she spends her time. Though she has dated other heartbreakers—like Joe Jonas—she's learned what to look for in a guy. One of the biggest things she needs is

a guy who understands her fame. "I steer clear of guys who have an issue with me having the spotlight," she said. "If someone I'm with gets really irritated when fans ask for my autograph, it's never going to work out. That's a definite red flag."

She's also gotten smarter about dealing with boys who are players. She knows the best thing to do is to get even. "If he doesn't call you for two days, just 'forget' to call him for two days," she explained. "You just didn't have time to call because he didn't have time to think about your feelings. You have to outplay the player."

"Mary's Song (Oh My My My)"

Despite dating a few losers, Taylor has never fallen out of love with love. She still believes that true love exists. One song that proves this is "Mary's Song (Oh My My My)."

"I wrote this song about a couple who lived next door to us," Taylor said. "They'd been married forever, and they came over one night for dinner, and were just so cute. They were talking about how they fell in love and got married, and how they met when they were just little kids. I thought it was so sweet, because you can go to the grocery store and read the tabloids, and see who's breaking up and cheating on each other or just listen to some of my songs, ha ha. But it was really comforting to know that all I had to do was go home and look next door to see a perfect example of forever."

"Mary's Song" is a tale about two kids who grow up together. They play in the backyard, and even beat each other up. Their fathers' joke that they'll end up falling in love, while the moms roll their eyes. The song follows the two kids through their first kiss and first fight and an eventual marriage proposal. It's a story above a love that passes the test of time. At the end of the song, Taylor sings: "I'll be 87; you'll be 89/I'll still look at you like the stars that shine."

This song, though based on a real couple, also illustrates Taylor's obsession with love. "I'm fascinated by love rather than the principle of 'Oh, does this guy like me?'" she said. "I love love. I love studying it and watching it."

Taylor shows she's a hopeless romantic when it comes to her taste in movies. Her favorite film is *Love Actually*. "My favorite scene is when Keira Knightley's character opens the door and this guy who has always been in love with her uses all these handwritten signs to confess that he loves her — without saying a word," explained Taylor. "It's beautiful."

Maybe the right guy hasn't come along for Taylor yet—a guy with signs proclaiming his love—but she's not giving up hope. She believes there's a happy ending waiting out there for her too. "I'm going to meet somebody someday who is so wonderful, and I'm not even going to remember the other guys," she said. "Later on, I definitely want to fall in love and get married and have kids. I believe in love completely, wholeheartedly."

"Our Song"

Taylor's first boyfriend inspired not one song but two. "Our Song" is also based on Taylor's first relationship when she was 15. She wrote "Our Song" for the ninth grade talent show. "When I wrote that song, I was dating this guy who was going to be there at the talent show," Taylor told the *Reading Eagle*. "And we didn't have a song. I thought I'd just sing it in front of everyone at the high school. He was my first boyfriend, and no one at the school had heard me sing, ever. It helped me fit in, I guess."

The song came easily and quickly to Taylor. "I wrote it in twenty minutes literally; I just got this idea of a song that was sort of like a story but was more conversational in the verse," she said during an GAC interview. "And I just started ad-libbing it, and I had to go back and remember everything I said, and it took like four run-throughs to write that song."

"Our Song" won over fans because many couples look for a favorite song to call their own. It may be the song they first heard together while driving in the car or the soundtrack of their first dance. Finding a song is difficult at times, but it's a fun part of a relationship that listeners can identify with and appreciate. Because of its fun theme and strong use of banjo, country music stations played it often. "Our Song" landed the No. 1 spot on Billboard's Country Songs chart for six weeks and actually made history. Taylor was the youngest country singer to write and sing a No. 1 song on that chart.

The song lyrics are unique in that they rely on metaphors to bring about meaning. A metaphor is a comparison of two unlike things that does not use the words "like" or "as." In the song, Taylor wrote, "Our song is the slamming screen door, sneaking out late tapping on your window," and "Our song is the way you laugh." The couple's song does not have to be an actual musical tune; instead, the song can be made up of all the sounds of their relationship, a door slamming, a laugh, or saying "Man, I didn't kiss her, and I should have."

The "Our Song" lyrics are also a good example of a subliminal message, an understanding that comes unconsciously to the listener. It is no mistake that "Our Song" is the very last track on *Taylor Swift*. "I wanted it to be last on the album, because the last line of the chorus is 'play it again'," she said. "Let's hope people take it as a hint to go ahead and play the album again."

Despite crossing over to the pop genre, Taylor has not forgotten her roots. Along with Charles Kelly, Faith Hill, and Dave Haywood, she paid tribute to country music at "We're All for the Hall," a benefit concert for the Country Hall of Fame in October 2009.

Taylor Swift, Deluxe Edition

■ Taylor rereleased her self-titled album in November 2007 with four bonus tracks—three songs and an important phone call she wanted to share with her fans.

Track 12, "I'm Only Me When I'm with You": Though she never specified whether this song was about a real or imagined relationship, the song does explains what Taylor wants in a boyfriend: someone she can be herself with. "The guy I'm looking for is the guy I can be me around, not a version of me I think he'd like," she told *Seventeen*. "He's the guy I'm not wearing different clothes for. I'm not holding back jokes because he might think they're stupid. I'm not afraid to show emotion because I might scare him. It's important to not have rules about who the guy is: the rule should be about who you are when you're with him."

Track 13, "Invisible": Similar to "Teardrops on My Guitar" and "Stay Beautiful" the song "Invisible" describes a girl in love with a boy from afar. The lyrics state "We could be beautiful, a mircle, unbelievable instead of invisible." Taylor divulged the song was about the son of her parents' friends in Stone Harbor, New Jersey. "They were always at my house and their son was my age, and he would always tell me about other girls he liked," she explained. "I felt, well, invisible. Obviously. So I wrote that song about it."

Track 14, "A Perfectly Good Heart"—Like "Should've Said No" or "Picture to Burn," this song is about heartbreak. The lyrics ask the question "Why would you wanna break a perfectly good heart?" This song probably stems from Taylor's experiences with being hurt by a boy, especially when it's unexpected. "Bad boys know how to keep the chase going through the entire relationship, and you never know if you completely have them or not," she explained. "But the worst is when you think you finally went for the nice guy and he breaks your heart it's like, 'What gives?'"

Track 15, Taylor's first phone call with Tim McGraw: Before meeting Tim McGraw in person, Taylor actually spoke with Tim on the phone during a radio show. She finally got to hear what Tim thought of the song. "It was awesome," he said. "Except I didn't know if I should take it as a compliment or if I should feel old… The more I hear it—I don't know if it's true or not—I start taking it as a compliment." Taylor assured him the song was in fact a compliment. "Thank you for having good music and everything," she told Tim. "I swear I'm not a stalker."

The two chatted for a few minutes on air, and Taylor even hinted that she'd be a good person to open for him on tour, which later helped her land a chance to open for Tim and Faith's Soul2Soul Tour.

By the end of the phone discussion, Tim said, "You can write songs about me any time, Taylor."

Chapter Three

Fearless Is Fabulous

Not long after Big Machine Records released Taylor's self-titled album, she began talking about her next move. "There were about 10 songs that we left off the first album that I can't wait to put on the second album," she said at the time.

Choosing which songs to put on the second album was an important and difficult decision. After such early success, the pressure was on Taylor to succeed again. Because Taylor is a prolific songwriter—she has written over 500 songs—the process of compiling songs for the second album began with shortening her list of tunes. "I've got, like, 75 written, and we just have to whittle it down to whatever number of songs we want to put on the album, and start recording," she told *Unrated Magazine*. "The second album will trump the first. That's a guarantee."

And trump it, it did. Big Machine Records released *Fearless*, Taylor's second album, in November 2008. It debuted at No. 1 on The Billboard 200 as well as the Country Albums chart. According to Nielsen SoundScan, 592,000 copies of the album were sold in the United States within its very first week. Boasting rave reviews from music critics, *Fearless* was named one of the top ten albums of the year by both the *Associated Press* and the *New York Times*. *Rolling Stone* named it one of the top 50 albums of the year. It won "Album of the Year" at both the 2009 Academy of Country Music Awards and Country Music Association Awards and the 2010 Grammys. Four and a half million copies had been sold by January 2010.

Why was *Fearless* such an immediate success? For starters, a few of the album's singles like "Love Story" were already hits before the album was officially released. Maybe it was the way Taylor promoted the album. She not only held her *Fearless* release party on the *Ellen DeGeneres Show*, but she also brought her digital camera to the Country Music Television Awards and asked some of her fellow country singers to advertise her new album. "I have Hank Williams Jr., Brad Paisley, George Jones, George Strait, Miranda Lambert, Martina McBride, and Dierks Bently. All the artists I love were there, and I got them all to say, 'Taylor's album comes out November 11—go get it,'" she explained.

Or maybe it was luck; after all, the album includes 13 songs, and 13 happens to be Taylor's lucky number. The album also came out on November 11, the 11th day of the 11th month, a purposeful decision. "It's just the same number twice, so I figure it'll be easier to remember than other numbers," she said. "It's just kind of repetitive."

Most likely, though, it was Taylor's ability to put out a second album full of honest and heartfelt songs that speak to fans of all ages.

The title of the album, *Fearless*, is telling because Taylor takes a fearless approach to songwriting. Like the first album, the second album includes songs about Taylor's past relationships, especially one high-profile ex-boyfriend, Joe Jonas of the Jonas Brothers. There are many interpretations of the word "fearless," and Taylor kept this in mind when titling her album. "It's a big deal to title your album, so I wanted to make sure that it was the right call," Taylor said. "I started thinking about the word 'fearless' and what it means to me. It isn't that you're completely unafraid. I think fearless is having fears, but jumping anyway."

"Fearless"

One of the times when people feel most vulnerable is at the beginning of a romantic relationship. You're unsure if the other person likes you and uncertain where the relationship will go. You're afraid to be yourself on a first date, perhaps fearful you'll do something to turn the other person off. Taylor's song "Fearless", the first track on the album of the same name, explores this uncertainty of first date in a different way. Instead of being fearful, the song is about jumping head first into the relationship, even if you have no guarantee how it will work out. It describes the exhilaration you feel at the beginning of a relationship when anything is possible.

Taylor was alone on tour, not dating anyone, when she wrote "Fearless." "It's about the best first date that I haven't been on yet," explained Taylor. "I just try and put myself in the position of 'this is really happening,' and what would happen on the coolest first date." According to Taylor, a first date is when "your walls are coming down" and you're "fearlessly jumping into love."

The song is another way Taylor shows her obsession with love. She likes that love can be impulsive. "I think that you can't be too neurotic about love. You can't plan everything out," she said. "I think that one of the cool things about love is that the spontaneity of it is what makes it so magical. I think the coolest way to have a first kiss is when you're in the middle of a sentence, and you're rambling on about something, and the guy looks over and just kisses you, and you're not expecting it. Like, you're not planning that. That's not underneath a terrace, underneath the moonlight with a shooting star

running across the sky and everything's perfect. I think the perfection of love is that it's not perfect."

Taylor illustrates this spontaneity in the lyrics of the song "Fearless." She mentions how the little things catch her attention on the date, like "the way the street looks when it's just rained." She gets so excited she wants to dance with the boy "right there in the middle of the parking lot." Whether the boy runs his hand through his hair or later glances over at her in the passenger seat, the excitement is almost too much to bear as the night leads up to that first kiss.

The rain motif, which was evident in many songs on Taylor's first album, reappears on the second album, especially in "Fearless." Taylor sings, "and I don't know why but with you I'd dance in a storm in my best dress." A storm is usually seen as scary, but by pairing it with a dance, she puts a positive spin on a negative word. She likes the boy so much, she'd dance in the middle of a storm wearing her nicest dress. That's an exhilarating feeling.

In many ways, "Fearless" shows Taylor's ability to always bounce back from a bad break up. It shows she still believes in the possibility of love. "No matter how many break-up songs you write, no matter how many times you got hurt, you will always fall in love again," Taylor said.

"Fifteen"

Taylor's most personal song to date, "Fifteen," is the second track on her *Fearless* album. It's about the ups and down she and her best friend, Abigail Anderson, went through their first year in high school. It's about the year of her life when Taylor said she changed the most.

"Our lives absolutely changed," said Taylor about the song. "I walked away from love, and then I walked into a record label. I walked onto a tour, and that is how my story ended. Abigail, my best friend, got her heart ripped out, and I was there and went through it with her, but I am really glad that I was able to write it down."

"Fifteen" is so personal to Taylor, she actually cried when she recorded it. That's because it was also about her best friend. "I'm not likely to cry over something I've gone through, even if it's the worst breakup ever. Maybe I haven't had that break up yet. Maybe there will be a break up where I'll just cry every time I think of it," she said. "But the things that make me cry are when the people I love have gone through pain and I've seen it. 'Fifteen' talks about how my best friend, Abigail, got her

heart broken when we were in ninth grade and singing about that absolutely gets me every time."

High school is often the backdrop for experiencing first love, but sometimes first loves are not positive experiences. Taylor introduces this idea when she sings about the first day of high school, when the senior boys approach young freshman girls with pick-up lines like "You know I haven't seen you around before." Many of these guys prey on younger girls, and might even lie and say, "I love you" when they don't mean it. Taylor describes this situation with the line, "When you're 15 and somebody tells you they love you, you're gonna believe them."

In the song, Taylor is quick to point out that these high school relationships do not stand the test of time. After you grow up, you realize how unimportant they can be. The lyrics state, "But in your life you'll do things

A Matter of Time and Place

■ How long does it take Taylor Swift to write a song? Well, it depends on where she is when inspiration hits. "Sometimes, if I'm around my guitar, I'll write it really fast," she said. Although some songs, like "Love Story" came to her in twenty minutes, it usually takes Taylor twenty-five minutes to a half hour to produce a tune from scratch. "When I get on a roll with something, it's really hard for me to put it down unfinished," she noted.

An article once misquoted Taylor in saying she could write a song in only three seconds. That is not true. "I read it and I was like 'Man, that sounds so conceited.'" Taylor said. "It takes me relatively really quick amounts of time to write songs, but it's not three seconds…I cracked up when I read that. I was like 'Really? I didn't say that.'"

Taylor doesn't have a writing studio or a special desk at which to compose. All she really needs is her guitar. "I don't need anything around me to write songs," she told *Flare*. "I've learned to not be snobby about where I have to write. I've even written a song in an airport on a paper towel."

greater than/Dating the boy on the football team." Here, Taylor is saying that even though she swore she was going to marry the boy someday, she realized there was

Giving Teens a Voice

■ Taylor's song "Fifteen" seemed to accurately capture the mindset of the American teenager. So when Best Buy was looking for spokespeople for their @15 program—a way to connect with youth and value their opinions as consumers—they looked no further than Taylor Swift.

Taylor filmed an online teen service announcement for the program and, in it, she talked more about the pressures of high school. "I think when you first step into the doors of high school, and you walk in, there are seniors and juniors and sophomores, and then you - freshmen," Taylor said in the TSA. "You think you're all alone. When you're 15, you think you're the only person in the world feeling this way. You're not.

"Looking back at being 15, I wouldn't have changed anything," she went on. "If I had been popular, I would have been perfectly content with staying where I was...It just wasn't the cool thing to be trying to do anything different, and I think that caused me to spend a lot of time alone, and spending a lot of time alone gave me a lot of time to think, and having a lot of time to think allowed me to write songs.

"In high school, it's cool to be different," she added. "And the farther away you get from middle school, junior high, the more you realize that. In the real world, if you have something about yourself that's different, you're lucky. It's not a curse.

"Don't make high school everything," Taylor advised. "Because if high school is everything, then you've got a long life to live, and I'd like to think that the best years of my life are still ahead of me."

more to life than being popular with boys.

"Fifteen" is one of those songs that appeals to both young and old listeners. Girls near the age of 15 enjoy it because it describes how they currently feel about high school, love, and boys. But older listeners appreciate Taylor's lyrics as well. They reminisce about their own high school days and probably agree that they've come a long way since that time. In fact, they had "bigger dreams in mind."

"Love Story"

"Love Story," released in September 2008, was Taylor's first single from the *Fearless* album. It was inspired by Shakespeare's play *Romeo & Juliet*, which Taylor read during her freshman year of high school. She and Abigail actually watched the 1970s film version of the play in class and reacted strongly to it. "We remember thinking the guy in the movie was really hot, and so we were mad the whole time. We were like, 'No one like that exists; it doesn't happen,'" Taylor said.

Taylor and Abigail were also upset about the tragic ending: Romeo fakes his death using a sleeping potion, Juliet kills herself when she thinks Romeo is dead, and in turn, Romeo kills himself when he finds Juliet has stabbed herself. Taylor alludes to the characters Romeo and Juliet in the lyrics of her song, but she provides a happy twist on a sad story.

"Romeo and Juliet were always my favorite couple because they didn't care, and they loved each other no matter what," explained Taylor. "And it was always my favorite, except for the ending. So with 'Love Story,' I just took my favorite characters and gave them the ending that they deserve."

Taylor was inspired by the tragic play, but also by a boy she almost dated. Her parents and friends did not approve of him. "I really liked this guy," said Taylor. "And I introduced him to my friends and family and they didn't like him. They were like, 'He's bad news. I can see it in his eyes—he is a liar!'"

At first, Taylor didn't understand their reaction, and it was the first time she could understand the pain Romeo and Juliet felt; they fell in love despite the fact that their families were enemies. Taylor never did date that boy; instead, she used the experience to fuel her songwriting. "Love Story" tells the tale of two young people who meet and fall in love, although their parents disapprove.

The song is full of references to the play *Romeo &*

Juliet, from the balcony where Juliet stands, to the "ball gowns," to the "garden." The lyrics also boast a vivid metaphor and allusion all in one. The line "I was a scarlet letter" is a metaphor, in that Taylor compares herself to a letter. But 'scarlet letter' is also a literary allusion. In Nathaniel Hawthorne's *The Scarlet Letter*, the main character, Hester Prynne, must wear the letter A on her dress. It is a punishment to show the whole town that she is an adulteress because she cheated on her husband. Hester was made to feel like an outcast. Although Taylor's Juliet in the song "Love Story" has done nothing wrong, she is "branded" a bad person for liking Romeo.

Unlike the tragic play, Taylor's version of *Romeo & Juliet* ends with a marriage proposal. In this way, Taylor believes "Love Story" is an optimistic approach to love. "Say yes, and everything will be fine forever, and it will be perfect, and we'll have a happy ending," she said about the song's message. "You want a guy who doesn't care what anyone thinks, what anyone says. He just says 'Marry me, Juliet. I love you' and that's all I need to know."

According to Taylor, songs like "Love Story" balance out the other songs on the album that describe the pessimistic side of relationships. "I think it's important to keep both sides of that," she said. "You know, to kind of be a little skeptical of it, but then if you meet the right person, just to believe it will be perfect."

"Love Story" also has a happy ending in its success on the charts. Taylor's first single was soon on the Billboard 100 top ten and peaked at No. 1 on the Top 40 radio chart (Mediabase). It was another first for Taylor Swift. She was the first country artist to land a No. 1 song on the Top 40.

"Love Story" is the kind of song that also speaks to both young fans and old. Taylor has seen its impact on women of different ages in her audience. "I've got a group of seven-year-olds whose moms all took them to the show," she said. "There's a group of six 40-year-olds all wearing tiaras and holding sceptres and singing 'Love Story.' I really don't have just one age group."

"Hey Stephen"

Taylor is known for working the names of real boys into the lyrics of her songs. "Hey Stephen," the fourth track on the *Fearless* album, is a perfect example of this.

"People who have no idea that I have a crush on them won't find out through me telling them, but they will find out when they hear their name in a song," she told *The New York Times Style Magazine*. "There was this guy who opened a couple of shows for me on tour and I talked to him a couple of times, but he never knew that I liked him."

That guy was 24-year-old Stephen Barker Liles of the country band Love and Theft. Taylor actually encoded the name of this band in the lyrics of the song. When the album came out, Taylor had to face this crush head on. She sent him a text message and told him to check out that certain track on her CD. "He sent me back a long e-mail saying 'Oh My God,'" Taylor recalled.

This was a lot of fun for Taylor, who enjoys having to face the consequences of naming names. "It's always fun for me to put something on the album that is personal," she said. "Something I know I'm going to have to deal with when it comes out."

What did Taylor reveal to Stephen through the song? The lyrics describe the exhilaration of having a crush: "Cause I can't help it if you look like an angel/Can't help it if I wanna kiss you in the rain so/Come feel this magic I've been feeling since I met you/Can't help it if there's no one else/ Mmm, I can't help myself."

In many ways, "Hey Stephen" is a persuasive song. In it, Taylor gives Stephen all of the reasons he should consider dating her. She states "of all the girls tossing rocks at your window/ I'll be the one waiting there even when it's cold." And if this wasn't reason enough, she mentions she's a songwriter: "All those other girls/Well, they're beautiful/ But would they write a song for you?"

Musically, "Hey Stephen" stands out from other songs on the album because of its happy background rhythm. It's got a beat you can almost clap along to, or snap along to for that matter. Turns out, country singer Martina McBride's daughters and their friends, about 10 kids total, actually served as guest performers on the track. "We were recording in her (McBride's) husband's studio, and they were hanging out," Taylor explained to *USA Today*. "We just hauled them all into the studio, put a microphone on them and had them snap their fingers to the end of the song."

So what did the real Stephen think of the song? Although Taylor and Stephen are just friends, he was flattered. "I think everyone would agree she's a total sweetheart and anyone would be lucky to go out with her," he said.

Like fellow country singer Kellie Pickler, Taylor writes songs about the harsh realities of love, exemplified in the tune "White Horse."

"White Horse"

Whether she was begging for a bedtime story or seeing a Disney film, Taylor enjoyed fairy tales as a child, and she's still fascinated with them today. And as a self-proclaimed hopeless romantic, she cherishes all of the images related to fairy tales, like a princess, a white horse or even a castle. But after experiencing life and love, she's come to understand that real relationships do not always end happily ever after.

"I think I'm very fascinated by the differences between reality and fairy tales. When we're little, we read these books and we see cartoons and the bad guy is always wearing black. You always know who he is," she said. "But in real life, the bad guy can be incredibly charming and have a great smile and perfect hair. He says things that make you laugh and he's sweet and he's funny, but you don't realize he's going to cause you a lot of pain."

The song "White Horse" is a perfect example of this difference between reality and fairy tales. Taylor wrote the song after a hurtful experience with a boy. "One time when I was hopelessly, helplessly, and tragically let down by a guy," she explained to *InStyle*. "Let down to the point where I was so hurt and felt so abandoned, like a damsel in distress, like this girl who thought she found Prince Charming and then ended up in the pouring rain. I just wrote what I felt about that and I came up with the song 'White Horse.'"

In addition to blending sounds of guitar, piano and cello, Taylor and her co-writer Liz Rose also placed common, vivid fairy tale images throughout the chorus of the song. One image is of a woman being swept off her feet and being carried up a stairwell. Another is of a white horse, perhaps one ridden by Prince Charming, galloping in to save the damsel in distress. The lyrics also allude to Hollywood, a reference to the movie capital of the world. The films made there often illustrate an unrealistic version of love and perfect endings.

The song uses these images to tell a broken fairy tale, where the girl does not get the guy in the end. In the lyrics, the girl calls herself a "stupid girl" and admits she is not the princess, nor is he Prince Charming, and the relationship is doomed: "It's too late for you and your white horse to come around."

Coming to this realization—that the perfect relationship you wanted is in fact, not perfect—is painful, and Taylor sings of this pain in the line, "I was a dreamer before you went and let me down." Through this line, she admits she's not only disappointed but she's been changed by the experience. She doesn't see love the same way anymore. Her dreams have been shattered.

Although the theme of "White Horse" is that fairy tales do not come true, the song ends with a bit of hope. Taylor vows, "I'm gonna find somebody someday who might actually treat me well," and at the end of the song, she's leaving the "small town" for the "big world," even watching her past fade behind her in the rearview mirror. She's off to explore bigger and better things. And she even taunts the boy with the line, "Try and catch me now."

The song "White Horse" originally was not slated to appear on Taylor's *Fearless* album. Because she believed there were enough "sad" songs on the album, she planned to put it on her third album. But that changed when her Los Angeles agency set up a meet-

The "Write" Words

■ Good writing—whether it's a short story, poem or song—is descriptive. And good writers like Taylor Swift use very specific details in place of common words. These include naming a specific color, brand or type. For example, in "Tim McGraw" Taylor states it's not a simply a truck but a "Chevy" truck. Below are a few ways Taylor used vivid description in the songs on *Fearless*.

"Fearless": Instead of saying the town is "small," Taylor calls it a "one horse town."

"Love Story": Instead of using the words "summer time," Taylor wrote "balcony in summer air."

"Hey Stephen": Instead of saying, "of all the girls who like you," Taylor says "of all the girls tossing rocks at your window."

"You Belong with Me": Instead of referring to "one night," Taylor sings "It's a typical Tuesday night."

"Tell Me Why": Instead of saying "I really need you," she uses the simile "I need you like a heartbeat."

"The Way I Loved You": Instead of saying "it's late," Taylor states "It's 2 AM."

"The Best Day": Instead of saying "When I was little," she says "It's the age of princesses and pirate ships and the seven dwarfs."

ing with *Grey's Anatomy* producers Shonda Rimes and Betsy Beers. The medical drama is Taylor's favorite show; she catches most episodes on her tour bus, watching them on DVD.

Taylor played "White Horse" for Shonda and Betsy, who both loved the song and wanted to play it on an episode in September 2008. "You should've seen tears streaming down my face when I got the phone call that they were going to use that song," Taylor told *Billboard* magazine. "I have never been that excited. This is my life's goal, to have a song on *Grey's Anatomy*. My love of *Grey's Anatomy* has never wavered. It's my longest relationship to date."

Because the song aired on *Grey's Anatomy*, Taylor decided to put "White Horse" on her *Fearless* album, much to her fans' delight.

> *"This is my life's goal, to have a song on* Grey's Anatomy. *My love of* Grey's Anatomy *has never wavered. It's my longest relationship to date."*

"You Belong With Me"

Inspiration comes easily to Taylor. She's been inspired by a neighborhood couple, the simple sparkle in a boy's eyes or a well-known play with a tragic ending. One time, she was even inspired through eavesdropping. The simple act of listening in on someone else's conversation led to one of her biggest hits, "You Belong With Me."

While on her band's bus one day, Taylor overheard one of her band members talking on the phone with his girlfriend. "The guy was going 'Baby, of course I love you more than music," Taylor recalled to *Self*. "'I'm so sorry. I had to go to sound check. I'm so sorry I didn't stay on the phone with you.'"

This clip of a conversation made Taylor's head spin, and the very first lines of the song "You Belong With Me" formed immediately. Taylor felt sorry for the guy because his girlfriend was yelling at him. She ran to her tour bus to write the song. "I elaborated the story and related it to another situation because I don't have a crush on a member of my band," she explained. "But I do know what it's like to want someone who's got someone who takes him for granted."

In some ways, "You Belong With Me" is very similar to Taylor's other songs like "Teardrops on My Guitar," "Stay Beautiful," and "Invisible" because it's about a girl

who longs to be with a boy she cannot have. He has a girlfriend and does not know how she feels about him. The girl featured in "You Belong With Me" is obviously in love with her best friend. She knows what makes him laugh and seems to be able to cheer him up when he's down. She knows "all his favorite songs" and even listens to his dreams. But she also sees the negative effect his current girlfriend has on him. His smile "that can light up this whole town" has disappeared because the girlfriend has brought him down.

In "You Belong With Me," songwriters Taylor Swift and Liz Rose rely on an effective use of punctuation: the question mark. The lyrics are full of questions, with lines like "Why can't you see?" "Hey, isn't this easy?" "Hey, what you doin' with a girl like that?" "All this time how could you not know?" and "Have you ever thought just maybe you belong with me?" These questions, popping up at various points of the song, help make "You Belong With Me" more conversational in tone. The questions, directed at the boy, are a message from the girl to the boy. The use of the word 'Hey,' a term people use to get someone's attention, also adds to this conversational tone.

"You Belong With Me" also compares the different types of girls in a school setting. There are the popular, beautiful ones who are on the cheerleading squad, who wear high heels and short skirts, and then there are the ones who wear T-shirts and sneakers and sit on the bleachers. Taylor compares the two types of girls in the song and by doing so, highlights another element of pain from her youth. "There were queen bees and attendants, and I was maybe the friend of one of the attendants," Taylor once said about junior high. "I was the girl who didn't get invited to parties, but if I did happen to go, you know, no one would throw a bottle at my head."

Taylor and fellow country singer-songwriter Clay Walker both got their lucky break as teenagers; a local radio station played Clay's demo tape when he was just 16 years old.

Singer-songwriter Colbie Caillat not only co-wrote the song "Breathe" with Taylor, she also sang back up vocals.

Thanks to it's great background beat and familiar topic, "You Belong With Me" climbed to No. 1 on the Mediabase Top 40 radio chart and Billboard Radio Songs chart. Taylor made history once more for being the first country singer to have two No. 1 songs there; "Love Story" was her first. The crossover hit was nominated for Song of the Year for the 2010 Grammys. The video for the song—in which Taylor played both the nerdy admirer and the popular girlfriend—won Best Female Video at the 2009 MTV Video Music Awards.

"Breathe"

Sometimes, a relationships ends, and it's no one's fault. Even if the guy wasn't a jerk, the break up still hurts. That's what Taylor wrote about in "Breathe," the seventh song on the *Fearless* album. It's a song she wrote with pop singer-songwriter Colbie Caillat.

Taylor actually requested the opportunity to work with Colbie. She heard Colbie's albums *Coco* and *Breakthrough* and became a big fan. "I fell in love with the way she makes music," Taylor said of Colbie. "I contacted her management right away, and I asked if I could write with her and sure enough, Colbie had a date coming up in Nashville where she was gong to be playing a show, and she had the day off."

"Breathe" is another song about heartbreak, one so painful it's hard to even breathe. "It's a song about having to say goodbye to somebody, but it never blames anybody," said Taylor. "Sometimes, that's the most difficult part, when it's nobody's fault."

Taylor and Colbie illustrated this with the line, "We know it's never simple, never easy, never a clean break." In other words, break ups are hard and complicated. But it's nobody's fault because "People are people and sometimes we change our minds." Sometimes, relationships just end.

The lyrics of "Breathe" show Taylor and Colbie's unique approach to songwriting. They infuse the lyrics with similes, like "Music starts playing like the end of a sad movie" and "You're the only thing I know like the back of my hand." It also boasts an image of struggle, with the line, "Every bump in the road I tried to swerve." The line is a metaphor for all the "bumps" or troubles the girl tried to avoid before the break up.

Perhaps the most emotional part of the song is the bridge, where Taylor and Colbie sing, "It's 2 AM, feeling like I just lost a friend/I hope you know this ain't easy

It all Starts with a Line

■ Where do Taylor's songs come from? How does she start the process of writing? Often, when writing a song, just one line comes to Taylor's mind, and she builds an entire song around that one meaningful phrase. Here are a few of the lines she said got her creative juices flowing:

"Fifteen": "Abigail gave everything she had to a boy who changed his mind"
"Love Story": "This love is difficult but it's real"
"You Belong With Me": "You're on the phone with your girlfriend she's upset, going off about something that you said"
"Tell Me Why": "I took a chance, I took a shot. And you might think I'm bulletproof but I'm not."

for me." Writing a specific time like 2:00 AM is a great detail. It implies late night anxiety; perhaps the break up is even affecting sleep. It's the late night/early morning when people lay awake at night and process painful emotions.

"As human beings, what we can't have is what we replay in our head over and over again before we go to sleep," Taylor told *Allure*.

"Tell Me Why"

Taylor said that songwriting is a form of therapy and that her album is like her diary. For example, the song "Tell Me Why" was actually inspired by a moment when Taylor was ranting and raving out loud about a guy she didn't officially date." He would say things that would make me go, 'Did you just say that?'" Taylor said. "It bothered me so much because he would say one thing and do another."

Taylor got so upset about these mixed messages that she went to Liz Rose's house to complain about the mind games. "[Liz] said, 'What would you say to him right now?' And I said that, "I'm sick and tired of his attitude, and I feel like I don't even know him. He tells me one thing and does another." explained Taylor. "We turned it into a song. It was so therapeutic."

More Secret Messages **Revealed**

■ Taylor encoded more secret messages in the lyrics of her *Fearless* album. If you've already decoded these messages, here's another challenge: decode the secret message hidden within the secret messages. Below, find the random capital letters and write them down in the order they appear to answer the question.

What song by another artist does Taylor wish she'd written?

"Fearless": i loved you before i met you
"Fifteen": i cried wHen recording this
"Love Story": sOmeday ill find this
"Hey Stephen": love and Theft
"White Horse": all i ever wanted was the truth
"You Belong With Me": love is so bliNd you couldnt see me
"Breathe": im sorry im sorry im sorry
"Tell Me Why": guess i was fooled by your smile
"You're Not Sorry": she can have you
"The Way I Loved You": we Cant go back
"Forever & Always": if you play These games were bOth going to lose
"The Best Day": god bLess andrea swift
"Change": you maDe things change for me

Answer: Hot N Cold (By Katy Perry)

plained Taylor. "I think getting mad is always your first reaction when something hurts. And you shouldn't feel bad about that," she told *Seventeen*. "Every person you date is different and makes you feel differently. Sometimes you can shake it off and you're fine—and then with another person, it can really affect you. It's the unpredictability of love that really scares us, but it's also what draws us into it."

Like "White Horse," the song "Tell Me Why" is full of negative images but ultimately ends on a hopeful note. After all the fighting and being mistreated, Taylor sings, "I take a step back, let you go/I told you I'm not bulletproof, now you know." From this line, it's clear she is ready to move on.

"You're Not Sorry"

The song "Tell Me Why" is unique in that the lyrics are full of references to an actual, physical fight. In one line, Taylor and Liz wrote, "You took a swing, I took it hard" and in another, "You tell me that you love me then cut me down." Other fight-related words include "bullet proof", "push me around," and "temper."

In this way, the song rehashes all of the horrible moments in the relationship; moments when this guy made Taylor feel "small" and made fun of her dreams. The guy may have even called Taylor a hurtful name, something she implies in the line, "I remember what you said last night."

All of these episodes are enough to make Taylor angry, though. She feels "confused" and "frustrated" and eventually says "I'm sick and tired of your attitude."

Anger is a normal part of a bad relationship, ex-

Another song about the pain and hardships of relationships is "You're Not Sorry." It's a song about realizing it's time to end a bad relationship. You're ready to give up and move forward.

"It is about this guy who turned out to not be who I thought he was," explained Taylor. "He came across as Prince Charming. Well, it turned out Prince Charming had a lot of secrets that he didn't tell me about. And one by one, I would figure them out...I wrote this when I was at the breaking point of 'You know what? Don't even think you can keep on hurting me.' It was to a point when I had to walk away."

In the lyrics, Taylor flat out tells the boy not to call her anymore: "I won't pick up the phone," she promises. She knows the guy will keep calling to say he's sorry, but she also vows not to believe him like she did last time. This

Taylor wrote "Forever & Always" about her ex-boyfriend Joe Jonas (center), who performs in the Jonas Brothers, with his siblings, Nick (Left) and Kevin (Right).

time "it's the last straw," a common phrase similar to "the straw that broke the camel's back." It's the point where everything has changed, and you can't go back to the way it used to be. With the line, "You used to shine so bright, but I watched all of it fade," it's clear she realizes this guy was not Prince Charming. Taylor also repeats the word 'no' several times throughout the song, which shows the relationship is indeed over.

"The hardest thing about heartbreak is feeling like you're alone, and that the other person doesn't really care...But when you hear a song about it, you realize you're not alone—because the person who wrote it went through the same thing."

A song like "You're Not Sorry" is hard to write and hard to listen to at times because it's about a break-up, but there's a need for break up songs, according to Taylor. "The hardest thing about heartbreak is feeling like you're alone, and that the other person doesn't really care," she told *Seventeen*. "But when you hear a song about it, you realize you're not alone—because the person who wrote it went through the same thing. That's why songs about heartbreak are so relatable. When you miss somebody, and you hear a *happy* song, it just makes you mad."

Another version of "You're Not Sorry" exists, and it's quite different than the version on Taylor's *Fearless* album. When Taylor appeared as the character "Haley" on one of her favorite shows *CSI*, "You're Not Sorry" was remixed with a new background beat. In this version, many of the lines from the song are repeated and have an echo, haunting effect.

"The Way I Loved You"

Confusing, complicated relationships can cause a lot of pain. But sometimes, these messy relationships make for exciting experiences. Girls say they want to date a nice guy, but sometimes, these nice guys are boring. That's the idea of Taylor's song "The Way I Loved You," track number 10 on *Fearless*.

"I got this idea for a song about being in a relationship with a nice guy who is punctual and opens the door for you and brings you flowers...but you feel nothing," said

Taylor. "The whole time you're with him, you're thinking about the guy who was complicated and messy and frustrating."

Taylor brought the title and the idea for the song to fellow songwriter John Rich, and together the two wrote "The Way I Loved You." The verses of this song describe the "perfect" guy, a guy who is "sensible," "incredible," "endearing," and "charming;" a guy who opens the car door and says, "You look beautiful tonight."

This guy may be nice, but the girl can't stop thinking about a past relationship with a not so perfect guy. The chorus of the song describes how she misses, "Screaming and fighting and kissing in the rain;" she misses "breakin' down and comin' undone." The relationship with this other guy was exhilarating, full of ups and downs. Taylor and John bring this idea about with the line "It's a roller-coaster kind of rush."

Despite the ups and downs, there was something special about that messy relationship. It was full of a lot of feelings, both good and bad. The messy relationship was emotional, evidenced by the lines, "I never knew I could feel that much" and "You're so in love that you act insane." In other words, sometimes love can make us "insane," make us crazy enough to do stupid things. But it's this emotion, this excitement, that we sometimes remember most fondly.

"Forever & Always"

Perhaps Taylor's most publicly discussed song on *Fearless* is its eleventh song, "Forever & Always," a tune Taylor admitted she wrote about ex-boyfriend Joe Jonas.

Fearless, Again

■ In October 2009, Taylor re-released her *Fearless* album, a platinum edition boasting six new songs and lots of bonus material.

"I decided to re-release my album *Fearless* because on one hand, there are people who are just discovering my music right now, but then on the other hand, there are people who have had this album for a year now," Taylor explained in an AOL interview. "So I have this scope of exactly what I think these albums should sound like. And when I write a new song, if I feel like it's more in the category of *Fearless* rather than my next album, I put it in a pile. I wanted to put out these songs—a lot of them I wish I could have put on *Fearless*—but now I get to kind of re-release it and put these songs on it."

The *Fearless* Platinum edition includes these new songs: "Jump then Fall," "Untouchable," "Forever & Always" (piano version), "Come in with the Rain," "Superstar," and "The Other Side of the Door." It also includes the music videos for her hit tunes "Change" and "The Best Day" as well as music videos and behind-the-scenes footage for "Love Story," "White Horse," and "You Belong With Me."

A photo gallery from her 2009 *Fearless* tour and the video for "Thug Story", a rap she performed with T-Pain for the CMT Awards, rounded out the platinum edition extras.

In the summer of 2008, it was rumored Taylor and Joe, the middle brother of Disney's the Jonas Brothers, were an item. Taylor appeared in *Jonas Brothers: The 3D Concert Experience*, a concert film released in February 2009. The paparazzi spotted the two stars together at the 2008 MTV VMAs, and later outside a trendy Asian restaurant called Tao, located in New York's Midtown. Joe was seen in the front row of Taylor's concert and vice versa.

Neither Taylor nor Joe confirmed or denied the relationship, but after their two-month courtship ended, Taylor let her fans in on the big secret. While hosting her *Fearless* release party on *The Ellen DeGeneres Show*, Taylor told the audience and everyone tuning in at home how Joe had broken up with her. "When I find that person that is right for me…he'll be wonderful," Taylor said "And when I look at that person, I'm not even gonna be able to remember the boy who broke up with me over the phone in 25 seconds when I was 18."

Taylor explained that after she got off the phone with Joe, she looked at the call log on her phone and saw 27 seconds. "That's got to be a record," she said.

This bad experience—being broken up with over the phone—inspired Taylor to write a last minute song for her forthcoming *Fearless* album. Just before the album was set to be finished, she squeezed in the tune "Forever & Always." It was something she felt compelled to do.

"I'd never had that happen to me before that way, with that abruptness. I thought to myself, 'This needs to be said,'" Taylor explained. "It's a song about watching somebody completely fade away in a relationship and wondering what you did wrong and wondering why things have changed."

The lyrics of "Forever & Always" are aggressive: "Did I say something way too honest/That made you run and hide like a scared little boy?" And they retell some of the very details of Taylor and Joe's break up with mentions of the telephone: "I stare at the phone/He still hasn't called." But once again, it's the use of questions that gets Taylor's message across. With lines like "Was I out of line? Did I say something way too honest?" and "Where is this going?" Taylor illustrates her confusion about the relationship, not knowing why it ended or what she did wrong. There are still many unanswered questions.

"Forever & Always" is also an example of how the rhythm of a song can support the meaning of the lyrics. When Taylor sings the line, "So here's to everything coming down to nothing," the notes of the song become staccato, broken up into detached, separate beats. The relationship is "coming down to nothing" and breaking apart just like the notes and the rhythm are broken up in that section of the song. Another part of the song where the notes and words mirror each other is the bridge. Taylor sings the words "Back up, baby back up" a bit more slowly, holding the vowel sound 'a' a bit longer as well. This sound mimics the emotion of going backward. This line is also an

Taylor's mother, Andrea Swift,
inspired the song "The Best Day."

example of alliteration; the consonant B is repeated with the words "back" and baby."

After Taylor announced her break up on *The Ellen DeGeneres Show*, Joe Jonas responded. It was rumored that he cheated on Taylor with *10,000 B.C.* actress Camilla Belle. "I never cheated on a girlfriend," Joe Jonas wrote to his fans via the Jonas Brothers' blog. "It might make someone feel better to assume or imply I have been unfaithful, but it is simply not true."

Joe and his brothers, Nick and Kevin, fought back a little in the lyrics of their song "Much Better." It includes the line "Have a rep for breaking hearts/Now I'm done with superstars/And all the tears on her guitar." This obviously refers to Taylor Swift because she is the one who wrote and sang the song "Teardrops on My Guitar."

> ## "She let me run from my pain for a little bit," Taylor recalled. "And I thought that was the nicest thing that she could have ever done."

Despite this, Taylor doesn't regret being honest about her relationship with Joe or writing a song about him. "You should never regret honesty," she told *Flare*. "Would I ever take it back? No. Because I've always been honest, I've always talked about whom my songs are about. To change that for the sake of a boy would be a shame."

"The Best Day"

There are many people in Taylor's life who have impacted her positively instead of negatively and her mother, Andrea Swift, is certainly one of those people. Taylor's folksy song "The Best Day," track 12 on *Fearless,* is actually a tribute to her mom.

Many of Taylor's fond childhood memories appear in the song, from a cold afternoon at a pumpkin patch to the day her mother set up a paint set in the kitchen. "In the first verse, I was talking about being five years old, so as a writer, it was really fun to go back to that place and the way that I used to talk when I was five," Taylor explained. "I wrote the song from that perspective, and I starting thinking, 'What would I be thinking if I was

five and I was remembering this?' And it goes, 'I'm five years old/It's getting cold and I've got my big coat on.' It had language like that—that makes me really think back to that time."

Taylor wrote the song alone, without the help of a songwriting partner. That's most likely because it was so personal, only Taylor could accurately tell the story of her childhood growing up in Wyomissing, Pennsylvania. In "The Best Day," she paints a vivid picture of her days as a kid, sprinkling the lyrics with details, like "pumpkin patch," "tractor rides," "Snow White," "princesses," and "pirate ships." In this way, she describes her home life as a land reminiscent of fairy tales. She even refers to the fact she grew up on a Christmas tree farm with the line, "I grew up in a pretty house where I had space to run."

But not every memory from Taylor's childhood is happy. During junior high, when she most felt like an outsider, she would often come home and cry to her mom about the mean girls at school. Her mom was always able to make her feel better. "You hold me tight and grab the keys," she states in the song. "And we drive and drive until we found a town far enough away/And we talk and window shop till I forget all their names."

These lines of the song are based on an actual moment in Taylor's life, when she called several junior high friends and asked them to go to the mall. All of the girls claimed they were busy, so Taylor went to the mall instead with her mom.

"We ran into all of them hanging out together in a store," Taylor explained. "I just remember my mom looking at me and saying 'You know what? We're going to the King of Prussia Mall!' which is the best mall in the whole state."

Even though Taylor and her mom drove a whole hour to shop at this mall, the experience made Taylor feel better. "We had the time of our lives," she said.

It was this moment when Taylor realized how much she appreciated her mom, who let her process her sadness in her own way. "She let me run from my pain for a little bit," Taylor recalled. "And I thought that was the nicest thing that she could have ever done."

With such sweet and heartfelt lyrics, the song proved to be a unique Christmas present for Taylor's mom. "I actually wrote that song without telling my mom and recorded it without telling my mom. Complete secret session," explained Taylor. "Then I got the track back and synced up all these home videos of me when I was a little kid and made this video and played it for my mom on Christmas."

Andrea Swift's reaction to the song and video was emotional. "She had no idea that it was me singing for the first half of the song," Taylor explained. "And then she just broke down crying when she realized I had done this whole thing to surprise her. It was a really cool moment."

"Change"

One of the most inspirational Taylor Swift songs is the last song from her *Fearless* album. "Change" is about believing in success even when it seems impossible. And once again, it's a song with very personal ties to Taylor's life.

"I wrote this song about being on a small record label, being a 16-year-old girl, and having a lot of odds stacked up against all of us," Taylor explained to *Country Aircheck*, according to GAC TV. "[It was about] having a bunch of big companies on Music Row that had a lot more room in their buildings and a lot more employees than our 12. A lot of people, if given those odds, would say that's not going to work."

It's true Taylor was once an unknown star on an unknown record label. Although Big Machine Records president, Scott Borchetta, had decades of experience in the business, he could not guarantee the success of his new label. Taylor knew a small record label might not be able to give her perks, like favors from other artists. She said she knew it would be "an uphill climb." In many ways, Big Machine Records was the underdog. "Being on a little record label, you have to fight harder than being on a bigger record label to be on award shows, to be a performer and a presenter, and to get big tours and support," Taylor told *Billboard* magazine. "My record label had 12 employees when I put out my album and my single, and I just kept looking around and thinking, 'Some day we are going to grow, and this is going to change, and we are going to have a fighting chance.'"

Things absolutely changed. Taylor became a music sensation, and Big Machine Records grew to become one of the most respected labels in Nashville, representing other stars like Trisha Yearwood and Jack Ingram. The specific moment of inspiration for the song "Change" came to Taylor after she won the Horizon Award—a highly coveted prize—at the 2007 Country Music Awards.

"I looked over at Scott Borchetta after I won, and he was crying," Taylor said. "That's when I finished [the song], because I knew I couldn't finish it until something like that happened. It was absolutely the most amazing night of my life, getting to see the emotion of all the people who worked so hard for me. So I wrote that song about that."

Within the lyrics of the song "Change" is an inspirational message for listeners. The beginning of the song depicts a sad time when the "final blow hits you," but the chorus later offers hope the situation will change if only you fight back. Taylor calls it a "revolution" when "these walls that they put up to hold us back will fall down."

With it's "you can do it" theme, it's no wonder the song "Change" was part of the official soundtrack for the 2008 Summer Olympics. Taylor's dad was actually the one to suggest pairing the song with the Olympic games. NBC played "Change" while showing highlight footage from the Olympics. During that time the song was available for download on iTunes, with proceeds going to Team USA.

Taylor's life has certainly changed in the last few years. She went from unknown songwriter to a country music and pop superstar. No matter what the future brings, though, she assured her fans she'll never change so much that she loses who she is at heart.

"I want my fans to know that I'm the same girl I was when the first album came out," she said. "I'm just not in high school and I have a different schedule. I feel the same things. I feel the same way. And my song are where I'll never hold back."

Limited and
Special Edition LPs

■ In between the release of her self-titled album in October 2006 and the release of *Fearless* in November 2008, Taylor released three special-edition albums, containing either new songs or alternate versions of old songs. These include:

1. *Sounds of the Season: The Taylor Swift Holiday Collection* (October 2007) This CD included an eclectic mix of six songs: two traditional songs, "Silent Night" and "White Christmas;" two festive and fun tunes, "Last Christmas" and "Santa Baby;" and finally, two original songs, "Christmases When You Were Mine," which she co-wrote with Liz Rose and her producer, Nathan Chapman, and "Christmas Must be Something More," a tune she wrote and performed for Christmas services at Bausmen Memorial United Church of Christ in Wyomissing, Pennsylvania.

2. *Live from Soho: Taylor Swift* (January 2008) For this iTunes exclusive album, Taylor recorded live versions of eight songs—"Umbrella," "Our Song," "Teardrops on My Guitar," "Should've Said No," "A Place in this World," "Mary's Song (Oh My My My)," "Tim McGraw," and "Picture to Burn"—in the Apple Store located in Soho, New York City, a neighborhood known for art galleries and boutique shopping.

3. *Beautiful Eyes* (July 2008) This limited edition LP, available only at Wal-Mart stores, included two new songs Taylor wrote when she was just 13, "Beautiful Eyes" and "I Heart ?" It also boasted a new version of "Should've Said No" and an acoustic version of "Teardrops on My Guitar." The DVD featured all of Taylor's music videos as well as her "under the rain" performance of "Should've Said No" from the ACM Awards. A special video for "Beautiful Eyes," which used actual footage from Taylor's 18th Birthday Party, was also included on the DVD. The album charted on the Billboard 200 and also debuted at number one on the Country Albums chart, moving her first album, Taylor Swift, into spot number two. In other words, Taylor had both the number one and number two albums on the Country Albums chart in the same week. It was another historic achievement for Taylor Swift.

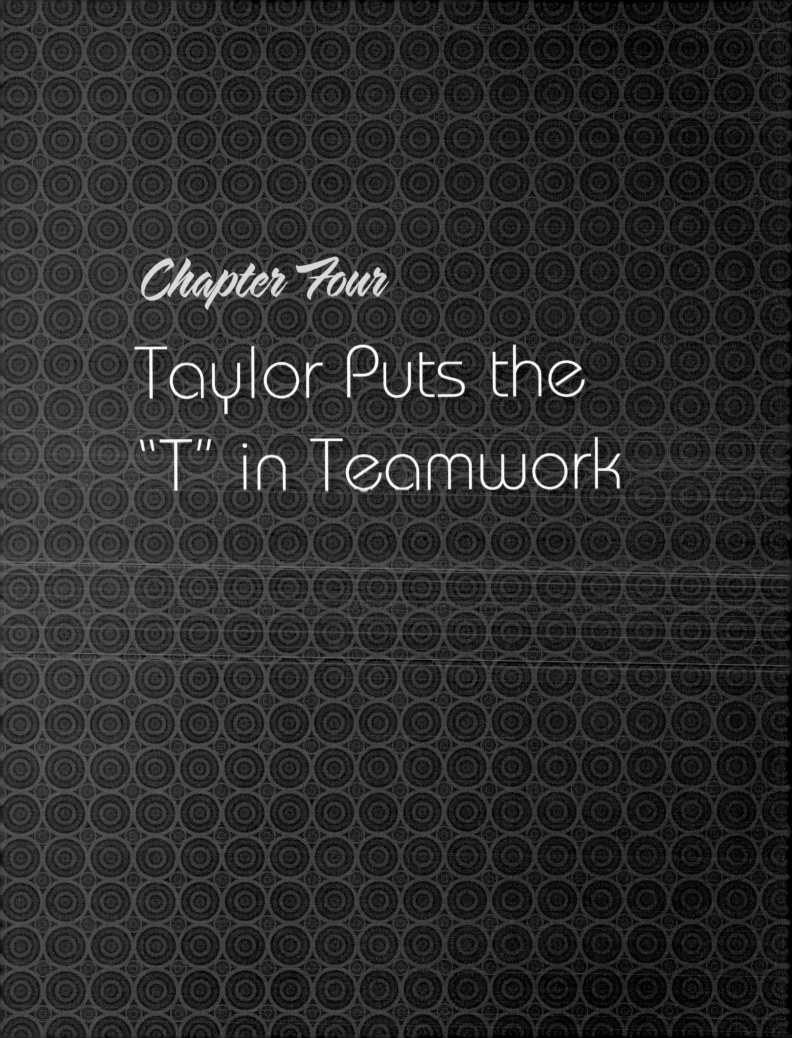

Chapter Four

Taylor Puts the "T" in Teamwork

They say writing is a lonely profession, but songwriting certainly doesn't have to be. Although Taylor has penned countless songs on her own, she's also enjoyed collaborating with other singers and songwriters. Whether it's her longtime writing partner, Liz Rose, or a one-time collaborator like Colbie Caillat, Taylor has proven that two heads—and sometimes three or four—can be better than one.

Liz Rose

Of all Taylor's songwriting partners, Liz Rose has co-written the most songs with Taylor. She co-wrote seven of the eleven songs on Taylor's self-titled album, including the hits "Tim McGraw," "Teardrops on My Guitar," and "Picture to Burn." She also helped Taylor write "Fearless," "You Belong With Me," "White Horse," and "Tell Me Why" from her *Fearless* album.

Taylor and Liz first started writing songs together when Taylor joined the staff of Sony/ATV as a songwriter. The two worked well together. "I love writing with Liz," Taylor said, according to *Songwriter Universe*.

"She'd write about what happened to her in school that day. She had such a clear vision of what she was trying to say. And she'd come in with some of the most incredible hooks." —Liz Rose

"When we write, I usually come in with a melody and some lyric content, and then we'll work on creating the rest of the song. She's a really good song editor."

Liz is equally enamored with Taylor. "My sessions with Taylor were some of the easiest I've ever done," she explained. "Basically, I was just her editor. She'd write about what happened to her in school that day. She had such a clear vision of what she was trying to say. And she'd come in with some of the most incredible hooks."

One of those hooks came from Taylor's math class, where Taylor daydreamed about her ex-boyfriend Drew and all the things she missed about him now that he was off at college. Taylor brought in her lyrics to "When You Think Tim McGraw" and Liz helped her perfect some of the lines at the piano. "Tim McGraw" ended up being Taylor's first single and the first of many hits songs for this songwriting duo.

So who exactly is Liz Rose? Her songwriting story is the opposite of Taylor Swift's. "I just kind of fell into it," Liz said. "I went into it backwards."

While Taylor began songwriting as a pre-teen, Liz didn't get into the business until much later in life. Liz got married at age 19 and had her first child by age 20. She had three kids in all and stayed home to raise them while her then husband, Johnny Rose, a music buyer and singer-songwriter, worked in the music industry. The Roses moved to Nashville to be in the midst of country music. After she and Johnny divorced, Liz worked in management for a while, even working for the country music duo Brooks & Dunn.

Then one day she went to a party and met a man named Ken Biddy, currently the president and CEO of Copperfield Records. Ken, who has a reputation for helping new songwriters develop their craft, saw emergent creativity in Liz Rose. He offered to not only hire her as a songwriter but also to train her. And soon, Liz boasted many songwriting credits. Working as a songwriter at age 37 came as a surprise to Liz because although she was always into music, she'd never considered the job. In fact, she'd never even written poetry.

By 1996, Liz started up her own independent music publishing company called King Lizard Music. She sold the company in 2001 to Jody Williams Music/Sony Tree and went on to work solely as a songwriter, co-writing country hits like "Songs about Rain" by Gary Allen, "The Wrong Girl" by Lee Ann Womack, and "Back of the Bottom Drawer" by Chely Wright. Other artists, including Trisha Yearwood, Tim McGraw, and Kellie Pickler, have performed Liz's songs. Liz said she is more of a lyricist than a musician because when writing

When Three is Not a Crowd

■ Most of the time, Taylor Swift and Liz Rose work exclusively together, but a few times, they've incorporated a third songwriter for extra creativity. For the song "Fearless," they teamed up with singer-songwriter Hillary Lindsey. For "Mary's Song (Oh My My My)," they collaborated with Brian Dean Maher.

Hillary Lindsey: Hillary is well-known for co-writing Carrie Underwood's first single "Jesus, Take the Wheel," which won Best Country Song at the 2007 Grammys. She also penned Martina McBride's "This One's for the Girls," "Stronger" by Faith Hill, "Men &

Mascara" by Julie Roberts, and "Seat Next to You" by Bon Jovi. She's also written songs for Miley Cyrus and Michelle Branch.

Brian Dean Maher: Brian wrote the top hits "You're Like Coming Home" by Lonestar and "Finding a Good Man" by Danielle Peck. He also wrote songs for Bering Strait and Rich McCready. Brian is the son of Brent Maher, a well-known producer in Nashville who has worked with Kenny Rodgers and Naomi and Wynonna Judd.

songs, she uses her brain rather than any particular instrument.

Liz's strong suit as a co-songwriter is her ability to serve as a therapist of sorts for artists struggling to find the right words. "I usually just write what-ever mood I'm in, or whatever's going on with whoever I'm in the room with," she explained. "I pick their brain and make them spill their guts! I think you have to have an open mind. I'm just lucky that, because I'm not an artist and I don't play, I can kinda go in a room with anybody and write. I'm the conduit; I'm there to help artists say what they want to say."

"I was just ranting and raving about how this guy is such a flake and such a jerk sometimes, and so cool other times," Taylor said. "I was like 'Liz, I don't know what's up with this guy.'"

This kind of "spill your guts" situation happened when Taylor came to a songwriting session upset about a confusing relationship with a boy. "I was just ranting and raving about how this guy is such a flake and such a jerk sometimes, and so cool other times," Taylor said. "I was like 'Liz, I don't know what's up with this guy.'"

In response, Liz asked Taylor important questions about her feelings, and the conversation turned into song lyrics. The two ended up writing "Tell Me Why" during that session, which appeared as track eight on her *Fearless* album.

Liz's songwriting gifts have not been overlooked by the industry. In 2007, she received the Songwriter of the Year award from SESAC (The Society of European Stage Authors & Composers), a publishing rights organiza-tion. Taylor actually helped announce and give the award to Liz. "She believed in me when I was a 14-year-old without a record deal," Taylor said at the ceremony, adding that Liz had always been one to give credit rather than take it.

SESAC also honored Liz in September 2009 for co-writing Taylor's biggest crossover hit "You Belong With Me." At this ceremony, Taylor and Liz showed their admiration for each other. "Thank you, Taylor," Liz said. "I love you."

"I love you so much," Taylor replied.

Today, Liz is on staff at Still Working Music, an independent music publishing company in Nashville.

What's her advice to budding songwriters? "Write the truth, write something you know, and write every day," she said.

Kellie Pickler

Kellie Pickler found fame through the television show *American Idol*. She appeared on Season Five of the show and worked hard to be one of the top six contestants. This honor allowed her to be a part of the *American Idol* Tour as well as embark on her own country music career. It was on that tour that she recorded her first album *Small Town Girl*. She soon joined Brad Paisley's *Bonfires & Amplifiers* tour, where she met Taylor Swift. Eventually, she opened for Taylor's *Fearless* tour. The two blondes are good friends despite their differences.

"People say we're such opposites, but that's what makes us such good friends," Taylor said of Kellie. "She's incredibly blunt. I love that about her."

Kellie said she admires Taylor's work ethic. "I've not seen many people work as hard as Taylor," she told *Rolling Stone*. "She's a very competitive girl, and those people go far."

Like Taylor, who writes about break ups and un-requited love, Kellie has used songwriting to work through difficult and emotional times in her life. Her song "I Wonder" is about her mother, who abandoned her when she was young. "The best therapy in the world to me is writing," Kellie said. "I can't express what writing has given to me—every sadness, every hurt, every tear, and every happiness. Writing works for me."

Kellie does not write every song she sings. But she always tries to identify with her songs, no matter who wrote them. For her self-titled album, she chose songs that reflected her life. "There isn't a single song on this

Anatomy of a Song

■ How do songwriters like Taylor Swift make sense of all those rambling thoughts, feelings, and ideas? They use a set structure to write song lyrics. Most songs include a chorus, several verses and a bridge. Taylor's crossover hit, "You Belong with Me," co-written with Liz Rose, boasts good examples of these elements.

Chorus: The chorus is the main idea or message of the song, and it's repeated many times throughout, as many as four or five times. The song's title is usually found within the lyrics of the chorus, often at the end. For example, the chorus of Taylor's Song "You Belong With Me" ends with those very four words

Verses: Verses support the chorus and often tell a story. They are detailed, specific and often set up a scenario. In the first verse of "You Belong With Me," Taylor describes a boy having an upsetting phone call with his girlfriend. Meanwhile, Taylor is in her bedroom listening to music his girlfriend doesn't like. The second verse goes even deeper into the story; it tells how Taylor and the boy go walking together and sit on a bench.

Bridge: This section is an additional verse that is shorter and different in rhythm and style from the other verses. Most songs have only one bridge. The bridge in "You Belong With Me" has a distinct, edgy beat. With the words, "Oh, I remember you driving to my house in the middle of the night/ I'm the one who makes you laugh when you know you're bout to cry," Taylor breaks down the familiar tune of the song with a bridge.

physically in the two years since my first album."

Just like Liz Rose listened to Taylor's troubles about boys, Taylor once served as a sounding board for Kellie. One day, during the *Bonfires & Amplifiers* Tour, Kellie came to Taylor's tour bus angry about an ex-boyfriend, who had actually gotten another girl pregnant. Taylor immediately thought there were song lyrics hidden inside Kellie's complaints. "There's no better way to get over something than to write it all down," Taylor advised.

So, the two country starlets sat in Taylor's tour bus bedroom and wrote "Best Days of Your Life," which appeared on Kellie's self-titled album. With lines like "And it's just too bad you've already had the best days/the best days of your life," the song is a "rub it in your face" kind of tune about the consequences of mistakes. "It's about how, for the rest of his life, he's going to regret cheating on her," Taylor explained. The song charted on both the Country Albums chart and Billboard Hot 100.

Writing the song was once again good therapy for Kellie. "You know what, I didn't think there was anything I could do to really get past that," she said. "But writing that song gave me complete closure."

It was also a meaningful experience for Taylor. They wrote the song in only thirty minutes. "It was so cool jumping into someone else's feelings for a minute and writing from their perspective," she said. "It was like I was writing my very first song. Exhilarating."

Unlike Taylor, Kellie never revealed the real name of the ex-boyfriend who inspired "Best Days of Your Life." But she did give this warning to future romantic interests. "You have to be careful when you date a songwriter," she told *People magazine.* "We always get the last word!"

John Rich

For "The Way I Loved You," track number 10 on her *Fearless* album, Taylor joined forces with John Rich, a man who needs no introduction in the country music world. John worked as a solo artist and a member of the band Lonestar before teaming up with Big Kenny for the country duo Big & Rich, known for the hit "Save a Horse (Ride a Cowboy)." In 2007, he released a second solo album, *Son of a Preacher Man.* John has co-written many songs for artists like Faith Hill and Tim McGraw. He has won the ASCAP (American Society of Songwriters, Composers, Authors and Publishers) Songwriter of the Year award three times and has served as a producer

record that I didn't live, that I didn't love," she said. "The hardest part was narrowing it down. The whole record is balanced—there's heartbreak, revenge, in love and happy, empowerment, and sassy songs. This record is an update of where I've been, emotionally, mentally, and

In a moment of writing therapy, Taylor penned "Best Days of Your Life" with friend and fellow country singer Kellie Pickler. The song appeared on Kellie's self-titled album.

Like Taylor, country singer John Rich is known for being "opinionated." The "Shuttin' Detroit Down" songwriter collaborated with Taylor for "The Way I Loved You," which appeared on *Fearless*.

and talent scout of sorts; he helped boost the country music career of Gretchen Wilson, who was once an unknown bartender.

John Rich's most controversial song thus far was "Shuttin' Detroit Down." In the midst of a national financial crisis, the federal government bailed out automakers as well as major banks on the verge of bankruptcy. The CEOs of some of these companies, however, still lived a life of luxury—flying in private jets, for example—after the bailout. "The CEO of Merrill Lynch took some bail-out money and spent a million dollars remodeling his office, and somewhere in the world found a $38,000 toilet and bought it for his office," John told *The Boot*. "I thought, 'Is this what this world has come to? There's a lack of reality and a lack of respect for American taxpayers.'"

John became so angry about the issue after watching the news, he wrote the song "Shuttin' Detroit Down." Like Taylor, John processes his emotions through songwriting. "I figured I had a choice," he said. "I could sit at home and be mad, or I could do what a country songwriter does—pick up a blank sheet of paper, a pencil and a guitar and write a song about it."

Taylor divulged it was always one of her objectives to write a song with John Rich; she appreciated that he was outspoken, something they have in common. She also admitted the pairing could backfire. "I had heard so many things about him. I just wanted to see what it was like to get into a room with him because I know I'm a very opinionated writer and I knew he was a very opinionated writer," she said. "So I knew this was either going to be the best thing in the world or was just going to be a complete train wreck."

The pairing worked, even though John was 35 and Taylor was 19 at the time; even though she wrote about high school crushes and he wrote about the economy. John said respect is a big part of the equation. "She knows herself and her audience very well, and she's so connected to who that audience is," he said. "She knows she's still a kid and embraces it. She writes things that are important to her. If she breaks up with a boyfriend, that's traumatic to her, and she'll write about it. Just like if I'm pissed off at the news, I'll write 'Shuttin' Detroit Down.' But we respect that about each other."

Taylor and John have a few things in common, besides being opinionated. For starters, they both fell in love with country music at a very young age. Taylor

Howdy, Partner!

■ Taylor has also worked with these talented singers/songwriters on both her first and second albums, as well as songs on her limited edition releases:

Brett James: After leaving med school, Brett became a Grammy-winning country artist, writing songs for Faith Hill, Bon Jovi, and Kenny Chesney. In addition to co-writing Carrie Underwood's "Jesus, Take the Wheel," he also co-wrote Taylor's song "A Perfectly Good Heart," which appeared on the special edition of Taylor's self-titled album.

Robert Ellis Orrall: Robert is a singer-songwriter who has enjoyed recording both pop/rock and country music. He co-wrote "A Place in This World," "I'm Only Me When I'm with You," and "Invisible" with Taylor. His original songs have been recorded by Reba McEntire and Collin Raye. He's also a record producer; in fact, he co-produced Taylor's self-titled album.

Angelo Petraglia: Known as the "fifth member" of the band Kings of Leon, Angelo is the co-producer of that group's albums. He also co-produced Taylor Swift's self-titled album and co-wrote "A Place in This World" and "I'm Only Me When I'm with You." Angelo plays in his own band, The Jane Shermans.

Troy Verges: Troy is the other co-writer of "A Perfectly Good Heart." He's also the author of countless songs, performed by Tim McGraw, Faith Hill, Bon Jovi, Celine Dion, Trisha Yearwood, and Martina McBride.

"It's just so unbelievable to see someone like Garth Brooks have kids who like my music," she explained. "I'm like, 'Are you kidding me? Your dad is Garth Brooks!' It's the coolest feeling ever."

fell in love with the song "Blue" at age six, and John had a similar experience. "The only thing I ever cared to do in my life, from the time I was 5 or 6 years old, is make country music," John said. "Country music is not a hobby to me. It's my DNA."

They also write very personal music, songs about their own lives. While Taylor wrote songs about her best friend Abigail ("Fifteen") or her mom ("The Best Day"), John wrote songs about his father and grandfather. And, there's one person they share the same opinion about—Garth Brooks.

"He is a living legend," Taylor said of Garth, best known for his song "Friends in Low Places." "If you asked me who my hero is, I'd say Garth Brooks."

Taylor even met Garth Brooks' daughters, who came to see her in concert. "It's just so unbelievable to see someone like Garth Brooks have kids who like my music," she explained. "I'm like, 'Are you kidding me? Your dad is Garth Brooks!' It's the coolest feeling ever."

John Rich is also smitten with Garth. He wants to write and record an album with the country music superstar. "If Garth would ever allow me to record him, to write a couple of songs and just stomp a hole through the floor in the studio with him, that would be a really big deal to me," John said. "I think he'd like me if he ever got to know me."

The Barlowe Brothers

Usually, songwriting collaboration happens face-to-face. Two or more people sit down to think, talk, and create lyrics. But one exception is Taylor's song "Untouchable," which appeared on her *Fearless* Platinum Edition. The song was originally written by Cary Barlowe, Nathan Barlowe, and Tommy Lee James and performed by the Barlowe brothers' rock music group, Luna Halo. In

2007, the song appeared on their debut self-titled album.

According to Nathan Barlowe, Big Machine Records president Scott Borchetta gave Taylor a copy of Luna Halo's album. Later, while performing on the show *Stripped*, Taylor covered the song "Untouchable."

"She could have chosen any cover in the world, but that's what she chose," Nathan Barlowe said. "We lucked out, really. She covered the song and it sounded amazing, so from there, there were so many YouTube hits on it and so many people watching it and doing imitations of it, that's when the label decided that they should put it on the record."

Taylor, who is used to writing or co-writing her own songs, changed the song to make it her own. Her version of "Untouchable" is different than the original; though the chorus is the same, the verses are different. "When I first heard it, it caught me off guard because I didn't even recognize the melody of the verse and some of the arrangement," Nathan explained. "But she's one of, if not the biggest artist in the world right now, and when she wants to change a little thing about your song, I'm fine with it, you know?"

Because Taylor changed the song significantly, she was given credit for co-writing the song. Interestingly, Nathan Barlowe has never met Taylor Swift, although his brother, Cary, did talk to her backstage at one of her concerts. In many ways, Taylor Swift boosted the songwriting and music careers of the Barlowe brothers and Luna Halo. For starters, the sales of their original version of "Untouchable" have increased. With the help of MySpace, they've gained new fans. People say to them, "I never would have found you without Taylor Swift." They've even gained some of Taylor's Swift's fans, who say, "I love your version" and "Where have you guys been all this time?"

The song's popularity also increased after Taylor performed "Untouchable" on *Saturday Night Live*. The Barlowe brothers watched her performance at the house of a friend, who threw a small party for the event. "I was just waiting for it anxiously," said Nathan. "And then

Taylor referred to country singer Garth Brooks as "a living legend."

Colbie Caillat is No. 1 on Taylor's "cool people" list; Taylor loves Colbie's album, *CoCo.*

when it came on, she looked amazing, and the setup was really beautiful, and I thought she sounded great on it. I was really happy."

Since the Taylor Swift collaboration, Cary and Nathan Barlowe have started to do more songwriting in country music. They are hoping the Taylor Swift connection helps them succeed. "I think having somebody like Taylor do your song, the respect level goes up," Nathan said. "A lot of people are curious to see if we can repeat the magic somehow, and we are, too."

Colbie Caillat

In 2007, Colbie Caillat entered the music scene with her first album *CoCo*, which debuted at No. 5 on the Billboard Top 200 Albums chart. Her song "Bubbly" was No. 1 on the Billboard Adult Top 40 chart and stayed there for 14 weeks. Another song "Realize" was also a top hit. Colbie, who grew up in California and Hawaii, said her songs are "optimistic" because she grew up having an easygoing lifestyle, listening to Bob Marley and Jack Johnson. "I'm happy," Colbie said. "And that gets expressed in my music."

Colbie quickly caught the attention of not only music fans but also other artists, especially Taylor Swift. After Taylor heard *CoCo*—which she called "this amazing album that I've fallen in love with"—Taylor knew she wanted to write a song with the album's singer-songwriter. After a phone call to Colbie's management, Taylor learned Colbie would soon be in the Nashville area and even had a day off for a songwriting session.

The two wrote the song "Breathe" for Taylor's *Fearless* album, and Colbie even sings backup vocals on the release. "I've got this awesome tape of us both singing it, and I'm playing guitar and she starts singing these backup vocals and I'm like, 'Oh my God, she's got the best voice ever,'" explained Taylor.

The Colbie duet is one of the reasons Taylor was excited about the release of *Fearless*. "I think she sounds beautiful on it," Taylor said of "Breathe," which was nominated for Best Pop Collaboration with Vocals at the 2010 Grammy Awards. "I'm so excited to have her voice on my album."

Although the relationship between Taylor and Colbie was initially just business, the two became friends. They share an admiration for each other. Taylor called Colbie "No. 1 on my cool people list." She even made a guest appearance during Colbie's interview for an A&E

Private Sessions video. "I have loved getting to know you and I consider you to be one of my close friends," Taylor said to Colbie. "Writing a song with you that went on my album was one of my favorite experiences with you."

"She's just one of the most talented people in every way that I have ever met. I am fascinated by her."
—Colbie Caillat

Colbie seems to feel the same way about Taylor. "She's so cute," Colbie said. "Taylor, she is one of my good friends. She's just one of the most talented people in every way that I have ever met. I am fascinated by her."

During the interview, Taylor prompted Colbie with a fill-in-the-blank sentence. "As you know, I am pretty fascinated by love," Taylor said. "Finish this sentence: Love is…"

It didn't take Colbie long to answer. "Love is something you have to find in yourself and in every person around you," she noted. "And it's something that takes time to get to know with them."

It's no wonder Taylor and Colbie are good friends. They both write and perform songs about love, and both seem to use songwriting as an outlet for emotion. For both artists, songwriting is often spontaneous. "I just let stuff build up inside of me, and I'll write three songs in a weekend," Colbie explained. "It's like this release. I don't pick something to write about. When I'm playing guitar, a melody comes out and whatever words come out, I go along with that."

The two young women also have a story in common; both were young when they fell in love with music and both started songwriting at an early age. Colbie's most relevant childhood moment was at age 11, when she heard "Killing Me Softly" by The Fugees featuring Lauryn Hill. "It made me want to start singing," Colbie recalled. "So I sang one of her songs at a talent show in sixth grade."

And like Taylor, Colbie also enjoys collaborating on the songwriting process. She wrote most of the songs on *Coco* with singer-songwriter Jason Reeves. The songs on her second album *Breakthrough*, which includes the hit tune "Fallin for You," she wrote with many other songwriters, including Kara DioGuardi, John Shanks, Makana Rowan, Rick Nowels, and Mikal Blue. Colbie also collaborated with Jason Mraz on the song "Lucky."

Taylor Songwriting Quiz

■ Test your Taylor IQ with this mini quiz about her songwriting quirks, bloopers, and habits.

1. **Where did Taylor write her hit "Love Story?"**
2. **Once, when Taylor was writing a song, her pen fell into the _____.**
3. **About how many songs has Taylor written?**
4. **After Taylor wrote a song on a paper towel in an airport bathroom, why did she get embarrassed?**
5. **Due to middle of the night song ideas, what does Taylor keep beside her bed?**

Answers: 1.) Her bedroom floor 2.) Piano 3.) About 500 4.) She was in the men's bathroom 5.) A recording device

Ever since Colbie Caillat co-wrote the song "Breathe" with Taylor, the two songwriters have been good friends.

Taylor's Favorite Songs and Songwriters

■ Taylor is not just a musician, she's a true music fan. Her musical tastes have changed over the years, though. Her first demo tapes, the ones she gave out on Music Row when she was 11, included the songs "There's Your Trouble" by the Dixie Chicks, "Here you Come Again" by Dolly Parton, "Hopelessly Devoted to You" by Olivia Newton John and "One Way Ticket" by LeAnn Rimes. Over the years, she's been inspired by meaningful lyrics and other songwriters' approaches to music. Below are a few of the songwriters and songs she admires.

Max Martin, "Hot N' Cold": "That song is just so brilliant melodically," Taylor said of the Katy Perry song. "And Max Martin is one of my heroes because he just knows how to craft these songs that get stuck in people's head, every time. He's brilliant. I think it's just pure pop goodness. I love that song."

Prince, "Nothing Compares to You": "I feel like there's a timeless thing that that song has," Taylor said of the song made famous by Sinead O'Connor. "It's just one of those songs where you know that when it was written, like 5,000 songwriters just put their pen down and went, 'Alright. I tried'...I think it's a brilliant song."

Alan Jackson: "You know who he is and you know who he stands for and you know what he believes in because his main goal is that he's always written about his life, and he hasn't really strived for the vocal acrobatics," Taylor said. "He hasn't tried to be anything but a guy who sings about his life. I realized...that's my goal. That's all I want to do."

Sheryl Crow: "I think she's great," said Taylor. "The candidness of her writing and how she tells it like it is, but still is vulnerable. I love that about her."

Brad Paisley: "I think he's a genius, the way he writes," Taylor said. "He can write something so touching it can make you cry, and then he can make you laugh so hard that you can't breathe."

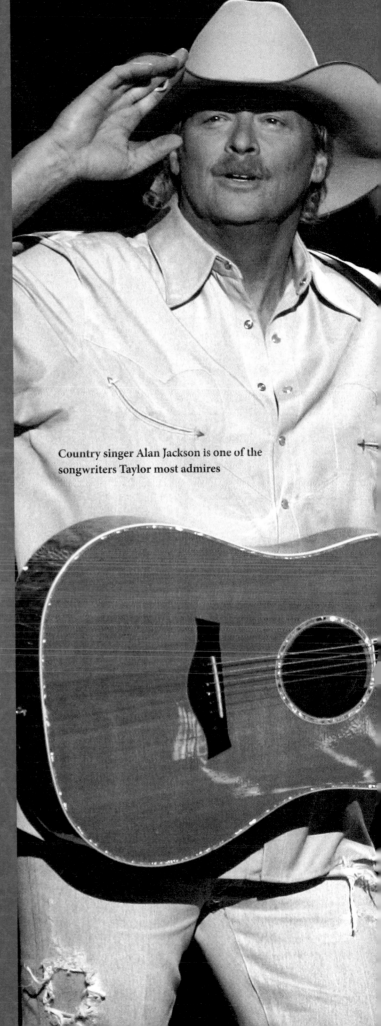

Country singer Alan Jackson is one of the songwriters Taylor most admires

Chapter Five

Beyond Lyrics: Taylor's Blogs, Journals, and More

Taylor Swift is an award-winning songwriter, but she also excels at other forms of writing, like blogs and journals. A lover of words, Taylor seems to choose writing as her first venue of expression. Whether she's posting her thoughts on her MySpace blog, journaling in her diary or simply writing a letter to a friend, words seem to come naturally to Taylor and ideas flow from her mind to the page almost effortlessly.

MySpace

Like her honest song lyrics, Taylor's MySpace page is very personal. Through regular posts on her blog, she shares the details of her fame, family, and feelings. The site is also a place for fans to listen to her music or watch original videos. It also updates fan on her calendar of events, TV appearances and concert venues. At the beginning of 2010, her total number of friends on MySpace was almost 1.8 million and her MySpace profile had been viewed almost 110 million times. MySpace, a social networking site originally launched in 2003, was a pivotal factor in Taylor's quick rise to fame, although she never intended it to be. Taylor simply grew up at a time when the social networking site became popular. In fact, she said her MySpace phenomenon was an accident.

"That was not a clever scheme," Taylor said in a *CMT Insider* interview. "I made a MySpace [page] in eighth grade because all my friends had MySpaces, and that's how they talked to each other. So I wanted to be cool, too, and I wanted to make a MySpace. And I happened to play music, so I made a music MySpace. I started uploading my demos to my music MySpace, and all of a sudden, I noticed that my friends were posting my music on their pages, and then their friends were hearing them on their pages and posting them on their pages. And all the sudden, I started to realize that I was getting friend requests from people I didn't know. So I was like,

'Hey, I'll accept everybody.'"

Soon Taylor had an Internet following—a fan base that grew once she released her first album and eventually began touring. Her MySpace page has not changed much since its beginning. The bio section—a spot where she tells fans about her toenails being five different colors because she can't make decisions—is written informally. "I wrote a bio, like a regular person bio," explained Taylor. "Not like an artist promotional bio, and that's how I've kept it."

Her blog posts are equally casual. Just like a "regular person," she writes about the weather, her friends, her favorite songs, foods she ate, places she went, things she did. For all the posts about everyday details, there are posts about a more glamorous lifestyle, full of award ceremonies, designer dresses, and worldly travels. She's famous, but when she writes about meeting another star at an event, she transforms into a gushing fan. Once, after she met Shania Twain backstage at the Country Music Association Awards, she wrote this on her blog: "She walked up to me and said she wanted to meet me and tell me I was doing a great job. She was so beautiful, guys. She really IS that beautiful. All the while, I was completely star struck. After she walked away, I realized I didn't have my camera. Then I cried."

Taylor's very first post, archived on the site, was written November 4, 2005. "So this is technically my first blog," she wrote. "So I think I'll make it about what's been going on lately. I've been in the studio every day recording for the album."

In this first post, Taylor also talked about a showcase she performed in front of Universal Records executives at Scott Borchetta's house. Since then, Taylor has maintained regular blog entries; sometimes she posts within a few days and other times, a few months go by without a new entry. She's never gone more than a couple of months without posting, however. Though her life has

changed dramatically since 2005, she's always been open and honest in her posts. From the beginning, she has thanked her fans in almost every entry. "I love you so much," she wrote in a 2009 post. "Thanks for making all of this a possibility for me."

Humor is another element characterizing Taylor's blog entries. She can be very funny. Once, she wrote, "I'm sitting in the production office of the Brad Paisley tour. That's right, I'm stealing wireless from Brad Paisley in order to write this." She often goes off tangent. She enjoys "free writing" and lets herself go on and on about something that is not necessarily important. It seems she can write about any subject, even the rain. Once, she wrote, "I'm here in Philadelphia, and it's raining and raining and raining. Oh, and there's wind, too. So, with all the rain added with the wind, you get sideways rain. And there's really nothing you can do about staying dry when there's sideways rain. Umbrellas only shield you from one angle, so you've basically got to give up on your hair. It's going to get wet. Same with clothes. With the added bonus of puddles, your shoes get totaled as well."

It seems no matter how many awards she's won or how many No. 1 songs she's had, Taylor still can't believe her own success. She often writes about this disbelief in her blog. "Part of me can't fully wrap my mind around the idea that this sort of thing could happen to me," she wrote in a December 2009 post, after learning she'd been nominated for eight Grammy Awards.

Thanks to MySpace and other online venues, songs can be heard or downloaded digitally. In this way, Taylor believes the Internet has made music more accessible to more people. "In this day of iPods and digital and Internet and the fact people can go get any music they want with the click of a button, I really think there are less boundaries and the lines are more blurred between genres," she told *The Star*. "And I think that's a beautiful thing."

Taylor is also prominent on another social networking site called Facebook. She had almost three million friends there by the beginning of 2010. Though she has more friends on Facebook than MySpace, the latter is where she posts personal blogs. Much of what is posted on her Facebook site are press releases or links to news events.

The Internet may have helped catapult Taylor's career, but there's a downside to having so much online attention. People post comments on Taylor's websites or other sites, and these comments are not always positive. A few people have even said "I hate her" or "She's ugly."

Deconstructing
Taylor's Posts

■ **Taylor puts her signature style into every MySpace blog post, whether it's the way she signs off or the way she shows emotion. Here are a few key elements her fans see in almost every blog update:**

Current Mood: These include inspired, anxious, imaginative, excited, and happy.
Hey: Taylor usually starts off her posts with the word "hey" and sometimes, it's spelled with two Ys.
CAPS: When Taylor wants to represent a mood visually, she usually types words in all capital letters, like EXCITED, AWESOME, HAHA, and BEST.
Random Letters: When Taylor wants to show excitement, she will attack the keyboard and type a bunch of random letters like, bdjsgfhadskfhkjdsh. This usually means she's so excited about something, she can't contain herself.
Excited: "I know that I use the word 'excited' in my blogs more than any other word in the English language," Taylor admitted.
Closing: Taylor always ends each post with "lovelovelove -T-"
Currently Listening: At the end of most of Taylor's posts, she usually states what song or album she is currently listening to. She provides an image of the album's cover and a link to Amazon. The artists Taylor listens to are varied and include Tom Petty and The Heartbreakers, Tim McGraw, Kings of Leon, Keith Urban, Kelly Clarkson, Rihanna, and Jewel, to name a few.

These can be upsetting to Taylor, though she tries not to read comments often.

"I try to put my focus on the ones who are saying things on MySpace because the MySpace comments are usually really nice," Taylor said. "They're from people who are just loving and sweet and kind and have wonderful things to say." In fact, MySpace comments have been able to lift Taylor's spirits in the past. "Going on MySpace immediately makes my day better. I may be thinking 'My hair doesn't look right,' 'I don't like this outfit,' or 'I need to do this or that,'" she told *Self*. "But when I log in, they're like 'Your music has changed my life,' 'Your music got me through this breakup,' 'Your song means so much to me.' When people are just constantly being loving to you, it's the nicest thing. It's just so cool. It's a constant stream of love."

Taylor does avoid reading comments, particularly those listed below articles or message boards where people are not required to provide their name in order to comment. Taylor believes anonymity makes people meaner than they normally would be. "On the Internet, it's very anonymous and you have every single opportunity in the world to bash anybody that you want to bash," she said. But Taylor has a good attitude about criticism. She understands music is

The New
Taylor Swift.com

■ Taylor's official website, www.taylorswift.com, used to have a journal-like feel to it. The pages looked much like a scrapbook; information appeared within the pages of a fake book on the screen. Shortly after Taylor turned 20 on December 13, 2009, her website matured, too. By late December 2009, the site had transformed from casual and charming to sophisticated and stylish. The new site featured glamorous photos of Taylor—with red lips and bold colored dresses—that pop out from a pure white background. Taylor is all grown up and so is her website.

The website features everything the old one did, including news, press releases, tour dates, and the like. But the new site features her MySpace blog posts more prominently and also boasts new pages, like Taylor Nation, a link to Taylor Swift merchandise, and Taylor Connect, a place for fans to interact online.

Taylor, pictured with Brad Paisley and Kellie Pickler has dealt with the down side of fame, like negative comments on websites.

subjective, which means it's a personal choice. "The beautiful thing about music is that everybody has an opinion about it," she said. "The thing that makes me value the people that like me are the people that don't like me, because if everybody liked you, then maybe you wouldn't value the people that really had your back all the time as much."

"If you read something about yourself, it makes you wonder what the public perception is of you," Taylor explained. "It makes you wonder if you look like a different person. And to be constantly questioning yourself is never good."

To avoid negative comments, Taylor said she doesn't receive Google alerts, e-mail updates about Internet activity related to her name. "If you read something about yourself, it makes you wonder what the public perception is of you," Taylor explained. "It makes you wonder if you look like a different person. And to be constantly questioning yourself is never good."

Instead, Taylor focuses her attention on her fans. To honor them, especially the fans who write loving messages to her on MySpace and elsewhere, Taylor actually reads their comments and tries to write back as much as possible.

The Video Diary

Video Blogs, what Taylor sometimes refers to as "video diaries," are a prominent feature on Taylor's MySpace page. Whether she's on tour, backstage, or shooting an episode of *Crossroads* with Def Leppard, she's usually recording everything that happens.

It's something she started doing at the onset of her career. In fact, her first blog post reveals how her parents gave her a video camera, which she took with to an event. "So basically I got to harass everyone nonstop for 12 hours," Taylor wrote. She has continued to record much of her life and travels, setting those videos to music before posting them on her site.

"Video editing has been one of my favorite things lately because you can take what happens in your life, and if you put it to music, it becomes this cool story, this cool visual," she said. "I never like to use my songs in the background. I always like to use other people's songs because I feel like if I let people in on my musical tastes

more, they'll know me more, and that's better, I guess."

Her videos are all over the board. In one, she watches the CMA Award nominations in bed. In another, she drives around a parking lot in a golf cart with her mom. Her band members are featured regularly. In one video, Taylor's bass player, Amos Heller, stole her headband. "We're sharing it," he said for the camera. Other videos showcase the many people behind the scenes, like sound and video guys, dancers, and parking lot attendants.

Taylor's video diaries often showcase her travels, the places she's visited, and the varied experiences she's had on the road. Taylor sees these places and experiences as an extension of the college classroom. Taylor has not attended college yet, but feels as though she has. "I've already gone to college...as far as being away from home, having to learn how to survive, having to learn so many different things about the (music) industry and meeting different people you've never met before," said Taylor, who has traveled to every state in the continental US as well as Europe and Australia. "It definitely rounds you out as a human being."

"It's good to have been places...to see Montana, to see Alabama...to see Nova Scotia," Taylor said.

On her blog, Taylor also posts photo diaries, collections of photos taken with her own camera. One of her January 2010 posts included black and white photos of her brother, friends, and band members.

Journaling

In many ways, Taylor's MySpace blog is a diary, but a very public diary available to her fans. She has also likened her albums to diaries. "*Taylor Swift* was the diary of my life from ages 14 to 16 years old," she explained. "And *Fearless* was the diary of my life ages 16 to 18. And my next album will be a diary from age 18 to that point in my life."

However, Taylor also keeps a private journal, where she writes her most personal thoughts, dreams, and desires. It's a habit she started when she was new to being a teenager. "I actually started writing in a journal when I was 13," she explained. "And I have them all in this safe in my house. I have like 25 of them because I would write every single night."

Taylor enjoys reading these old journals from time to time and reminiscing about old times. "It's crazy to go back and read them and think about all these things I once thought were so out of reach," said Taylor, who focused many journal entries on her goals. Her "goal sheets" from the age of 14 and 15 included items like winning a CMA award, having a No. 1 song, or being on the cover of *Seventeen* magazine. She's done all of these things and more.

Taylor continues to journal regularly to this day. In fact, a journal is something she carries around at all times. "My purse weighs, like, 50 pounds because my diary's in there and it weighs so much—it's the thickness of a Bible!" she told *Seventeen*. "I always have to have a diary or a journal with me wherever I go because I'm constantly writing stuff down, whether it's what happened to me that day, or an idea for a song in the middle of the night."

What does Taylor write about in her journal? Probably the same things she puts into her song lyrics or writes on her blog—like her family, friends, boys, and relationships. One thing is for sure: Taylor fills the pages of her journals quickly. She wrote about that fact in her MySpace blog after receiving a new journal as a gift from actress Kate Walsh. "Kate Walsh sent me a journal, and it was perfect timing because I was JUST about to run out of pages in my current one," Taylor wrote. "I don't know how she knew that. She must have magical powers."

A good place for Taylor to journal is on the road. While traveling, she tries to find time to write not only songs but diary entries. "I do love writing on the road," she said. "I usually write at the concert venue. I'll find a quiet place in

Taylor-inspired
Journal Writing Exercises

■ Journaling is a great way to relieve stress or work through problems. When something is bothering you, it's helpful to write down your frustrations. Journaling can also help preserve memories of times gone by. Try the following Taylor Swift–inspired writing exercises. For an additional challenge, practice free writing, allowing yourself to write for a certain amount of time without self-editing or re-reading what you wrote until you're finished. Free writing will insure your entry is honest and authentic. Set a timer for ten or 15 minutes, and write an answer to one of these thought-provoking questions:

Childhood Memory: In "The Best Day," Taylor wrote about her childhood growing up on a farm. Think back to when you were five years old, and describe a specific time when you felt happy, carefree, and safe. Remember to jot down sights, smells, and sounds from that event.

Lonely Experience: In the song "The Outside," Taylor describes how she felt like an outcast at school. Think of a time when you felt left out from a group. Describe the events that made you feel this way. How did you deal with the feeling of loneliness?

Disappointment: In "White Horse," Taylor sings about a fairy tale romance gone wrong. Think of a time when you felt disappointed in either someone or something. What happened that changed your opinion? How did you cope with the disappointment?

some room at the venue, like the locker room."

Journaling is a means of stress relief for Taylor. In addition to writing in her journal, she relaxes by lighting candles, listening to music, or painting abstract art.

Taylor's Tweets

In 2006, the social networking site Twitter was launched and quickly took pop culture by storm. Twitter serves as a quick, easy way to keep up-to-date with your friends and family, and in Taylor's case, her fans. Status updates are often concise and to the point; they can be about important things or just idle babble. Celebrities like Ashton Kutcher and John Mayer use Twitter regularly, and so does Taylor Swift. By the end of January 2010, Taylor had 2.5 million followers on Twitter.

Unlike MySpace, which Taylor said was an accident, Twitter was a purposeful decision for Taylor. "Twitter has just become big in the last couple of months," Taylor told *Whirl* magazine in 2008. "And, my dad's a stockbroker, so it's all about trying to figure out what's going to be huge tomorrow and getting in front of it...I always want to be on the cutting edge of all those platforms."

Just like Taylor writes her own posts on her MySpace blog, she always writes her own tweets on Twitter. "I absolutely am the only person who knows how to get into my Twitter," said Taylor, who posts under the name taylorswift13. "So it's all me."

Taylor likes the short format of Twitter and it's conversational advantages. "It's instant gratification," she said. "You can give people updates without having to blog. Also, you can tweet back and forth with other artists and fans."

In fact, Twitter is responsible for getting John Mayer and Taylor Swift together for the duet of "Half of My Heart" for his *Battle Studies* album. It started when John Mayer tweeted this: "Waking up to this song idea that won't leave my head. 3 days straight now. That means it's good enough to finish. It's called 'Half of My Heart' and

I want to sing it with Taylor Swift. She would make a killer 'Nicks' in contrast to my 'Petty' of a song."

Of course, Taylor read this tweet, and the seed for the duet was planted. "I freaked out when I heard, because I've been such a big fan of John for such a long time," Taylor told *Elle*. "I'm really excited about just the idea that he would even mention me in his Twitter!"

The two eventually recorded "Half of My Heart," which pays homage to the unique sound of duets performed by Stevie Nicks of Fleetwood Mac and Tom Petty. "If this is going to be my love letter to that style of music, who's going to be the Stevie Nicks in this equation?" John Mayer said. "And I thought, 'This Taylor Swift girl is going to be around for a long time.'"

> *"My dad's a stockbroker, so it's all about trying to figure out what's going to be huge tomorrow and getting in front of it...I always want to be on the cutting edge of all those platforms."*

The song was a hit. "Half of My Heart," turned out to be the most downloaded track from John's album. The song debuted at No. 25 on the Billboard Hot 100 singles chart and No. 12 on the Digital Songs chart.

Taylor's tweets, like her blog posts, are usually down to earth and character revealing. Here's a few of her best:
* "There was something really romantic about Polaroid cameras. I miss them and want them back."
* "Grocery stores are wonderful. I passed by these brooms that smelled like cinnamon. It was 100% winter. I was 100% happy."
* "Girl in the front row wearing a banana costume, I applaud you."
* "Cooking myself dinner while wearing glasses. I'm so, like, totally a grown-up right now."
* "Cooked all night with some of my favorite girls, then watched *CSI*. Then YouTubed videos of cute kittens. What can I say, I'm a thug."

* "When I drive past herds of deer, I always feel the need to caution them on the dangers of traffic, usually addressing them as 'Bambi.'"

* "Seeing 13's EVERYWHERE for the past few days. And 31's. Which is 13 reversed. Which totally still counts."

* "Just found my old life-size Brad Paisley cardboard cutout. Or better yet… It found me."

* "I'm twenty."

* "At the fancy hotel, I may have broken the fancy curtains because I didn't know they have a fancy electric button you push to close them. Hm."

* "Photo shoot all day, followed by dinner with Emma Stone. Then we wandered around a candy store like wide-eyed little kids."

* "About to put on my official *CSI* cast and crew hoodie for the flight. You know… From my old days playing a corpse and fighting crime."

The Art of Fine Writing

With so many people writing e-mails, blogs, and generally communicating via the computer, some people believe the art of fine writing, the days of paper and pens, are a thing of the past. True, Taylor uses MySpace and Twitter to communicate, but she loves stationary, and she often sends hand-written letters to friends. Once, she sent her backup singer, Liz (Elizabeth) Huett a card with a picture of a sad kitten on the front. Paper products, like cards and stationary, are something Taylor said she splurges on.

"There's this store called Papyrus, and they have these boxes of beautiful cards and I love them," she said in a *CMT Insider Interview*. "And another thing that I'm obsessed with right now is old-fashioned wax seals. You light it and it drips the wax and you have a little stamp thing. I love writing cards and letters to people, and I have all these different colors of waxes so it goes differently with different colors of the envelopes, and you just stamp it, and it's pretty."

Taylor likes stationary so much, especially glittery stationary, she said she'd splurge on writing supplies rather than buy a house in the Bahamas. "I don't need a house in the Bahamas right now," she said. "But I do need stationery."

Due to Taylor's love of stationary and cards, it's no wonder Taylor partnered with American Greetings. In fact, Taylor will create and produce her own line of greeting cards and stationary, as well as online greetings and personalized photo products. The line will launch in spring 2010.

"We are absolutely thrilled and honored to introduce Taylor Swift as the newest writer and creative contributor to the American Greetings family," said Zev Weiss, Chief Executive Officer at American Greetings. "Her abilities as a storyteller and songwriter make her a natural at writing cards for consumers of all ages. She has the unique ability to connect with her fans through life experiences and greeting cards do the same—cards help people express, connect, and celebrate these events with the important people in their lives. We believe it's a natural fit!"

The Taylor Swift cards will serve as yet another way for Taylor to illustrate her love of words. The cards will be inspired by her life and her personality. "My idea of a great song is a song that says how I feel better than I could. I feel the same way about greeting cards," Taylor said. "I've always been fascinated by feelings and how we express them to each other. Getting to write and design these cards is a wonderful experience."

Taylor's Autobiography

■ She's only 20 years old, but Taylor is already talking about penning an autobiography. She'd have a lot to say, especially in the later chapters, covering the events since her first album's release.

"Years from now it would be cool to write a book about all the crazy stuff and the insane things I've gotten to do," Taylor said. "I will write my biography for sure. My life moves so fast, I have to write it all down; otherwise, I can't remember where I was yesterday."

Considering all those journals she has locked up in a safe, Taylor already has a good start on that life story; plus, her blog posts and Twitter updates would serve to fill in any gaps in her memory.

Chapter Six

People and Places

Taylor Swift had the talent, creativity, and self-confidence to make it in the music industry. But she also had a great support system, made up of family, business partners, friends, and even fans to help her along the way. In addition to being encouraged by the people closest to her, Taylor was also inspired by her environment. The places she spent time—whether it was Pennsylvania, Tennessee, or the Jersey Shore—all played a part in her journey to stardom.

Taylor's Family

The heart of the Swift family is Taylor's mom, Andrea Swift, who has stood behind Taylor every step of her career. Andrea usually accompanies Taylor while she's on the road. Taylor's mom is a foundation of support for Taylor, but she's also a source of inspiration.

"Before she had me, she was this really big business

> ## "Before I make decisions, I always think, 'What is my mom going to think if I tell her this? Is my mom going to be really upset if she finds out that I did this?'"

executive who worked for an ad agency. I really look up to that," said Taylor. "I respect that she had a career on her own and lived alone. She had me when she was 30. She had a complete career of her own and was supporting herself."

Taylor described her mom as "rational" and "down to earth." It was Andrea Swift who taught Taylor the first rule of success: it doesn't come without hard work and dedication. "My mom always said, 'I don't feel like you just get discovered, there's a lot more that goes into it,'" Taylor recalled. "I want you always to have high hopes but low expectations.'"

In keeping with this theme, Andrea Swift never promised her daughter she'd be famous one day. She just told her to try her best, which Taylor always did. Over the years, the two became best friends. Although Taylor and her mom sometimes fight about the temperature of the tour bus—Taylor likes it warm and her mom likes

it cool—Taylor knows she can go to her mom with any problem and get honest advice. "She's always, always around," said Taylor. "She's the person in my life who will just literally look me in the eye and say, 'Look, snap out of it.' And I need that person."

Taylor said her mom has never been concerned with how many records she's sold or how many awards she has won. In an interview on *Loose Women*, a British talk show, Taylor even divulged that at award shows, her mom usually says, "Honey, you're not gonna win this one." In this way, her mom tries to keep Taylor grounded and not let success go to her head.

Taylor respects her mother's opinion. It's one of the reasons Taylor does not participate in rebellious behavior, like drinking or smoking. "I can tell my mom everything, and I do," she said. "Before I make decisions, I always think, 'What is my mom going to think if I tell her this? Is my mom going to be really upset if she finds out that I did this?' Usually I decide, 'No, I'm not going to go through with this.'"

Like most parents, Andrea Swift is protective of her daughter. For instance, she reprimanded Kanye West backstage at the 2009 MTV VMAs, after he interrupted Taylor's acceptance speech. When Andrea Swift reads negative comments or rumors about Taylor online, she's tempted to write back. "I'm going to make a name," Taylor's mom said one time. "I'm going to be TexasCutie425, and I'm going to go on there, and I'm going to tell them that that's not true, because that's not true."

Of course, Taylor told her mom not to get involved with online comments. "There's one rumor on there now," Taylor told her mom. "There's going to be 40 rumors on there by the end of the week."

While Taylor's mom offers Taylor strength and support, her dad, Scott Swift, brings enthusiasm, laughter, and business savvy. Taylor called her dad a "super fan." He is known to sell T-shirts and hand out guitar picks at her concerts. "He loves anything I do," Taylor said. "It is so cool to have someone so positive around who just gives me props for basically everything that I do."

Taylor called Scott Swift "the proudest dad you could have" because he's always approaching people to say, "Hi, I'm Taylor Swift's dad." For this reason, Taylor really enjoys showing her dad what she's been up to lately in the studio. "Playing new songs for my dad will always be one of the most rewarding things I get to do," she wrote in her blog.

Taylor's dad also has a great sense of humor. He's been known to do silly things, like ride a Segway around an arena parking lot or shout "Hey! That's Taylor Swift!" in public. Once, he followed Taylor around at an award show, picking up metallic pieces that kept falling off her bejeweled dress. Each time he found a new particle, he'd call out, "E-Bay!" as if planning to sell parts of his daughter's dress on the internet.

"He's a social butterfly and loves being on tour," Taylor explained. "He loves it so much, he thinks it's absolutely hilarious to mess with me and try to embarrass me as much as possible."

Despite his silly personality, Scott Swift is a wizard at money. As a financial advisor for Merrill Lynch, he has taught Taylor about the value of money since she was a kid. "My dad has been telling me all about my accounts and my finances since I was like two," she explained. "Before I could talk, he was talking to me about where my money was invested."

Taylor has taken her father's financial advice to heart. She's careful about her spending and tries not to splurge. "I don't like to make extravagant expenses unless it's putting back into my career," said Taylor, who used a big chunk of her earnings to purchase her own tour bus. She always meets regularly

Who is **Taylor's manager?**

■ Considering Taylor's busy schedule and lifestyle, you may wonder who manages her day-to-day affairs. Does she have a manager? "I don't really have a manager," Taylor divulged. "I have about five or six people who I really trust. I think it's important that I'm there at every single meeting. When I'm home, it's not playtime and fun games and days off. I'm at the management building every single day, planning our next step and organizing our next move. It's gotten to a place where it's like, well, do we really need a manager if it's all been us the whole time? … If it ain't broke … you know?"

Taylor doesn't need too much help staying motivated or keeping focused on her career. She's always been able to do that for herself, thanks to her competitive nature. "It has driven me to the place I am right now," she said of her character trait. "Sometimes it gets to be too much. I have never gotten to the point where I have been so competitive that it's been self-destructive. I think it's good to have a little competition in you, but not too much."

Taylor keeps her competitive side in check when it comes to friends who are also in the business, like Miley Cyrus of *Hannah Montana* or Selena Gomez of *Wizards of Waverly Place*. "I think it would be a real shame to disallow yourself from having a really cool friendship with someone just because she is in the same line of work," Taylor told *Flare*. "You can never prevent people from creating feuds in the media, but what you can do is control how you view competition. I just don't compete with other people; I compete with myself."

"There's also something very fascinating to me about the music business and about where the money is really made and the percentages and the point systems and things like that on records."

with a business manager to talk about money. And, it seems Taylor takes after her dad with an interest in finance. "There's also something very fascinating to me about the music business and about where the money is really made and the percentages and the point systems and things like that on records," she said. "It's something I've really taken an interest in lately."

In addition to her mom and dad, Taylor is supported by her brother, Austin, who is about two years younger. Like most kids, Austin and Taylor had their share of arguments as kids. "We used to fight like cats and dogs," Taylor said. "But when I went on the road, I started really missing him. I'd come back and he'd be four inches taller. So we started hanging out when I came home."

Taylor is amazed at how much her younger brother has grown up in recent years.

While Taylor left regular high school to be home schooled, Austin attended John Paul II High School in Hendersonville, where he played lacrosse. He was recently accepted to Notre Dame University after applying early. In fact, Taylor helped Austin tour the campus in the fall of 2009 before any decisions were made. The visit did cause a disturbance, though. The Swifts were on campus only a few minutes, when a large group of students started following them. Later, Taylor found out professors actually allowed the students out of class just to catch a glimpse of Taylor Swift. The experience certainly put a smile on Taylor's face, thanks to five enthusiastic students. "There were these guys—five of them—standing in a row with their shirts off," Taylor explained backstage at *The Oprah Winfrey Show*. "And they had painted 'ND' and then 'Hearts' 'TS' on their chests. Like each one of them was a letter, and I was like 'That's the coolest thing that's happened to me in

awhile.' It was very impromptu."

In times like this, Austin may find it difficult to be the brother of a famous music star. Because he probably needs his own space from time to time, he even moved into a room on the garage level of the Swift house. However, he's very proud of his sister. He took many pictures of Taylor on the road; these photos were included in the *Fearless* Platinum Edition album.

Austin also shares his dad's sense of humor and often makes Taylor laugh. Once, he called his phone and left this message: "iPhone, I'm sorry I lost you. But if you're listening to this, please come home. I miss you." Taylor thought this was so funny, she even tweeted about it.

Although Austin is not interested in pursuing a career in music, he does love music in general and even introduced Taylor to his "eclectic and cool" tastes. "He introduced me to Kings of Leon, things I wouldn't have ventured into," Taylor said.

Business Partners

Taylor has a supportive family, as well as a trusted songwriting partner like Liz Rose, but credit for her success as a singer-songwriter is also due to two business partners, Scott Borchetta and Nathan Chapman.

Scott Borchetta, president of Big Machine Records, knew there was something special about Taylor Swift when he first heard her sing during those early trips to Nashville. He was smart enough to keep in contact with Taylor's father and watch her grow as a musician. And, when she was 15 and played for him again, he knew it was time to cultivate this talented girl's potential. "She played some songs in our first meeting, and I was just killed on sight," Scott said. "She's the full package, somebody who writes her own songs, and is so good at it, so smart; who sings, plays the guitar, looks as good as she looks, works that hard, is that engaging and so savvy. It's an extraordinary combination."

Other executives in the country music industry thought Taylor was too young, but Scott knew her youth was her biggest asset. He knew her teen

Taylor and her brother, Austin, used to fight like "cats and dogs" but now have a great relationship.

The BFFs

■ Besides her family and business partners, Taylor relies on good friends to encourage, inspire, and support her. In addition to her pals and songwriting partners Colbie Caillat and Kellie Pickler, these are Taylor's closest girlfriends:

Abigail Anderson: Taylor has been friends with Abigail since they met in English class their freshman year at Hendersonville High School. The two loved to watch *Love Actually* during Christmas break and talk in silly voices inspired by the film *Napoleon Dynamite*. Taylor often visits Abigail at Kansas University, where Abigail is on the swim team.

Miley Cyrus: A country singer and star of the Disney show *Hannah Montana*, Miley is the daughter of country singer Billy Ray Cyrus of "Achy Breaky Heart" fame. Taylor visits Miley whenever she's in Los Angeles. The two also performed together at the 2009 Grammys. "We're friends, so anytime I'm performing with her, my nerves go away," said Taylor. "Cause she's always trying to make me laugh or is doing something ridiculous."

Selena Gomez: Selena stars on the Disney show *Wizards of Waverly Place*. "We talk all the time, almost everyday," Taylor said of Selena. "She's just such a cool person because she's so real, and a lot of times people get to a level where they're famous and people know them, people recognize them, and they become…less real."

Caitlin Evanson: Caitlin is Taylor's fiddler player, and the two have spent lots of time together in rehearsals and on the road. In fact, Taylor is good friends with all the members of her band, including Amos Heller, Elizabeth Huett, Mike Meadows, Grant Mickelson, Paul Sidoti, and Al Wilson. Taylor posts videos and photos on her blog that feature Caitlin. She tweets about her, too: "In furniture-browsing conversation, @caitlinbird just said 'Oh yeah, I saw that on the YouTube.' The unnecessary 'the' made me chuckle."

Demi Lovato: In addition to starring in the film *Camp Rock*, Demi also plays Sonny on the Disney show *Sonny with a Chance*. Taylor's a big fan of Demi's music. After seeing her video for "Don't Forget," Taylor sent Demi this message: "I just watched your new video and started crying. Hit a nerve. Watching again now. That's probably my favorite video ever."

Emma Stone: Emma starred in the films *Superbad* and *Zombieland*. Taylor and Emma do fun things together like go out to dinner followed by ice cream at Baskin Robbins. According to Taylor, the two also shopped at a candy store like "wide-eyed little kids."

perspective in songs about love, crushes, and break ups would attract fans outside of her age group. "She's a teen, but there's no bubblegum aspect to it," he said. "There's heartache in her songs and her voice. It feels fresh because the rawest heartbreak is probably the first heartbreak."

When Taylor signed on as his client, Scott Borchetta offered her something truly special: an active role in the production of her music. Taylor was involved with every aspect of the album, from writing the songs to choosing them. "And I'm proud to say, thanks to Scott Borchetta, every song on this album are ones I've written," Taylor wrote on her blog about the self-titled album. "Not

Actress Emma Stone of *Superbad* is one of Taylor's closest friends.

too many artists get to say that, and I thank God for putting me with people who love what I write and have the courage to allow me to have that much creative freedom."

> *"I thank God for putting me with people who love what I write and have the courage to allow me to have that much creative freedom."*

Even though Scott knew Taylor had great potential, he was surprised by her rapid success. "What I didn't know was how beautifully this flower would bloom," he said, according to *Country Standard Time.* "People don't just like Taylor Swift, they love Taylor Swift. I am so happy for her. And, she makes all of this so much fun."

In the past, Scott was also concerned about the impact Taylor's rise to fame would have on her. "My fear is that she'll conquer the world by the time she's 19," Scott once said after the release of *Fearless.* "She'll get to the mountaintop and say, 'This is it?' Because she's just knocking down all of these goals that we didn't even have for the first album…. My job at this point is really to protect her and not burn her out."

Taylor turned 20 in December 2009, but she hasn't showed any signs of burning out. In fact, with a third album due out in 2010 and more *Fearless* Tour dates on the calendar, she seems to be on a roll.

Another man responsible for Taylor's success as a singer-songwriter is Nathan Chapman, who produced many of Taylor's singles, including her first single, "Tim McGraw." He also co-produced her first and second albums. Taylor and Nathan have a long history together. "I've been working with Nathan Chapman, this amazing producer who's been producing my demos since I was thirteen," Taylor wrote on her blog several years ago. "He quote unquote 'gets me' and what I'm trying to say with my music."

Nathan, whose parents were Christian singers, grew up with a knowledge of the music industry. In college, he majored in English, an education he finds useful in songwriting, something he also does. In fact, Nathan co-wrote "Christmases When You Were Mine" for Taylor's holiday album, and has written songs for Martina McBride and Aaron Jones. Nathan has also produced the music of artists like Lori McKenna and Sara Evans, as well as his wife, singer-songwriter Stephanie Chapman.

Taylor and Nathan work great together, and their connection was a guiding force when it came time to produce Taylor's self-titled album. Nathan stood out from the other producers Taylor had worked with. "I got to record with a bunch of really awesome producers in Nashville," Taylor said. "But none of them sounded the way it did with Nathan…the right chemistry hit."

Taylor joined Nathan as producer of her *Fearless* album, which added another dimension to their business relationship. It also merited awards. The two won Album of the Year at the Country Music Association Awards in November 2009. "I felt pretty good," Nathan said after the big win. "It was nice to get an award like that. The music business is so hard and so tricky…this level of success would blow anyone away."

Taylor and Nathan were blown away again when they learned Taylor was nominated for eight Grammy Awards, including Record of the Year and Album of the Year, two nominations she shared with Nathan. It's sometimes hard for Taylor and Nathan to believe the success they've achieved in such a short amount of time. "I was talking to my producer, Nathan, today about everything that's happened this year. We were being nostalgic and going back to this time four years ago, three years ago, two years ago," Taylor wrote on her blog. "Now this year. We just…can't believe it. Earlier this week, he had a last-minute-get-over-here-right-now-and-celebrate party at his house, because the news had just broken: we were nominated for eight Grammys."

The news was so exciting, Taylor called Nathan immediately. "I remember…hearing the screaming voices of the drummer and the bass player and the mixers and publishers who helped put this album together," she recalled of the conversation. "He (Nathan) put me on speakerphone, and we all screamed together. I couldn't stop saying 'I love you' to them."

Taylor is once again working with Nathan Chapman for her third album, a fact that brings her peace of mind. In reference to a photo of Nathan Chapman,

Merry Swiftmas

■ How far would a fan go to show support for Taylor Swift? One fan, singer-songwriter Evan Taubenfeld, who used to play guitar for Avril Lavigne, wrote an original song inspired by country music's blonde-haired, blue-eyed cutie. His song "Merry Swiftmas (Even though I celebrate Chanukah)" was an Internet sensation in December 2009. He not only posted the song online, but tweeted it to Taylor.

In the song, Evan asks Santa for "a blonde who likes to sing." But not just anyone will do. In fact, with a great deal of creative rhyming, Evan snubs a number of other beautiful, famous women in his song, including Megan Fox, Scarlett Johansson, Amy Smart, Penelope Cruz, Lindsay Lohan, Cameron Diaz, Emma Stone, Angelina Jolie, and Britney Spears. Who's the lady of Evan's dreams? He gives his specific holiday request in the song's chorus: "Santa for my gift/Please send me Taylor Swift."

The song boasts some funny lines, like "No one will mess with her when she's mine/And Kanye will watch his mouth next time," which refers to the MTV Video Music Awards when Kanye West interrupted Taylor's acceptance speech for best female video. Another great line, hinting at a possible marriage between Evan and Taylor, is "I know her and I are gonna fit/Taylor Taubenfeld has a ring to it."

Of course, Taylor responded to Evan's song through Twitter. "This makes me smile," she wrote.

In "Merry Swiftmas," actress Megan Fox is snubbed in comparison to Taylor Swift.

Taylor wrote this on her blog: "Getting back in the studio with the same guys I trust and know and love."

The Fans

Whether she's winning an award or playing a concert, Taylor makes a point to thank her fans. She knows that without her fans—who bought her mega platinum albums and purchased tickets for her sold out concerts—her success would not be possible. They made her the superstar she is today.

Taylor fondly remembers the first time a fan recognized her. After landing at the airport in Boise, Idaho, a woman approached Taylor in the terminal. "Taylor, I just love your song and want to wish you great things in your career," the woman said. Taylor thanked the woman, but assumed her mom or label representative put the woman up to the stunt. The comment, however, was genuine.

"How did you know who I was?" Taylor asked.

"Because I listen to radio, and I watched your video," the woman replied.

Being recognized by a fan was such a confidence booster for Taylor. It warmed her heart as well. "This was the first time someone had actually KNOWN who I was and MY NAME," Taylor wrote in her blog. "I just walked over and hugged her and said, 'You're the first person who's ever done that, thank you.' It was an amazing moment to remember, and I always will."

Since then, Taylor has been spotted by fans all over the United States and beyond. Even fans in her hometown treat her like royalty. One day she was at her favorite restaurant, Cracker Barrel, and a couple approached her. "Will you please hold our baby?" the couple asked, before handing over a five-month-old child. "Sure, do you have a camera?" Taylor asked. But the couple didn't want a photo. "No, we just wanted to tell her some day that you held her," they said.

Taylor's fans are so important to her, she always finds time to write an autograph, take a photo, or just hold a baby. She understands this is a part of being famous. "It really bothers me when famous people get all mad when people ask for their autograph," she explained. "They are like 'Oh my God, my privacy has been invaded; everyone wants to talk to me.' This is what I asked for. This is what I've wanted since I was a little kid. I want to be known for my music."

Taylor's fans find some unique ways to capture Taylor's attention or show their appreciation for her music. One male fan gave her a turtle shell with her face painted on it. Fraternity guys often paint her name on their chests; sometimes, a male fan yells out "Marry me" during a set. Other fans have gotten her name, and even her autograph, tattooed on their bodies. When they meet Taylor, many of her fans cry. This doesn't bother Taylor. "I get a lot of criers, and I love criers because I like emotional people," said Taylor. "Some artists are very uncomfortable when people cry, but I happen to think it's the cutest thing on the planet when someone meets me and starts crying."

Taylor treats her fans like friends. She looks every fan in the eye, talks to them and gives every fan her undivided attention because she remembers what it was like to be a fan. "I went to concerts and I went through meet and greet lines, and I know what it's like to walk away and think that you didn't really make an impression on your favorite artist and that you were kind of just in a line," Taylor said. "I never want anyone leaving my concert feeling like I didn't appreciate them coming with everything that I have."

Because she doesn't drink, smoke, or do drugs and has led a very modest lifestyle in comparison to other stars her age, Taylor has been told time and again that she's

Taylor made her signature hand gesture—a heart—with the help of a fan.

a good role model for young girls. It's an honor Taylor takes seriously. Her young fans factor in to her musical and non-musical decisions. "Before I make a decision, I stop and think about the 10-year-old girl I saw last night at my concert in the front row," Taylor said. "I think about her mom. I think about how they bought my CD, thinking that I'm a good role model. Then I think about how they would feel if I did something to let them down. I can't imagine a greater pain than letting one of those mothers down. I honestly can't."

The Power of Place

Taylor is truly a product of her upbringing. She had loving, supportive parents and a solid education. She also grew up in three different towns and each played a part in shaping her life and career.

Her early years in Wyomissing, Pennsylvania, gave Taylor stability and safety. Growing up on a Christmas tree farm in this wealthy suburb, Taylor had space to roam and create. Wyomissing boasts all the perks of a small town with just under 12,000 people, but is still close to larger towns like Reading and Philadelphia. Despite social problems with friends at school, Taylor enjoyed her years in Wyomissing. She spent most of her formative years singing karaoke at contests and festivals. Many of her early songs about the pressures of fitting in, like "The Outside" were inspired by her experiences in Wyomissing. Taylor lived in Wyomissing until April 2004, when she relocated to the Nashville area.

While Wyomissing gave Taylor security, the Nashville area offered her opportunity. When she was 14 years old, Taylor moved to Hendersonville, Tennessee, located just 18 miles from Nashville. Hendersonville is much bigger than Wyomissing, with a population three to four times larger. Like Wyomissing, it offered Taylor a laid back suburban life style with a bigger city close by. Its beautiful location on Old Hickory Lake is rivaled only by its close proximity to country music capital. Nashville is where country music lives and thrives. It's also home to The Grand Ole Opry, a performance venue dating back to the 1920s with a rich past in showcasing country, bluegrass, and even gospel artists. Moving to Nashville was the right decision for Taylor's career, since she was able to work as a songwriter for Sony/ATV on Music Row and eventually get discovered by Scott Borchetta at The Bluebird Café.

One place not often mentioned in interviews with Taylor is Stone Harbor, New Jersey. Before moving to Nashville, Taylor's parents owned a summer home in Stone Harbor, located along the New Jersey coastline of the Atlantic Ocean. Taylor spent her summers there since she was two years old. "It was a pretty magical place to grow up," Taylor told *The Philadelphia Inquirer* about Stone Harbor, where she sang karaoke at open mic nights at restaurants and coffee shops.

The resort town served as an inspiration for many of her early songs. One called "Smoky Black Nights" was about life on the shore and another song, "Invisible," was based on a boy Taylor knew in Stone Harbor. The summer house was located on the bay, and her days there were full of typical summertime fun. The Swifts rode on Jet Skis, explored islands, looked for hermit crabs, and walked barefoot. "We used to all gather together on the dock when the boat parades would go by on July 4 and we'd shoot water balloons at them," Taylor added.

Taylor's other favorite Stone Harbor memories include the Italian Garden restaurant on 96th Street and Springer's Hometown Ice Cream, where Taylor usually got cookies'n cream or cookie dough ice cream. Another perk of Stone Harbor summers was a bird sanctuary across the street that Taylor viewed through binoculars. She also had her own clubhouse above the garage, painted and decorated in her own style. One summer, she wrote a 250-page novel. In this way, Stone Harbor was a place where Taylor discovered her authentic self, away from the popularity contest she faced at school in Wyomissing. "I was allowed to be kind of weird and quirky and imaginative as a kid," Taylor said. "And that was my favorite part of living at the Shore."

Taylor's Hometowns, **Side by Side**

	Wyomissing, Pennsylvania	Hendersonville Tennessee
Population, based on 2000 census	11,172	40,620
First settled in	1685	1778
Nearest major city	Philadelphia	Nashville
Schools Taylor attended	*The Wyndcroft School in Pottstown, PA *Wyomissing Area Jr. and Sr. High School	*Hendersonville High School *Aaron Academy (Homeschool program)
Other notable residents	Jon & Kate Gosselin of *Jon & Kate Plus 8*	Legendary musicians Johnny Cash and Conway Twitty

Taylor's Travels, Mapped

1. Wyomissing, Pennsylvania: Taylor was born here and lived on a Christmas Tree Farm until age 14.

2. Hendersonville, Tennessee: Taylor moved to this suburb of Nashville in 2004 to launch her career in country music.

3. Stone Harbor, New Jersey: Taylor spent her summers, from age two to 14, at a vacation home in this resort community.

4. Nashville: Home of Music Row, this is where Taylor's career got its jumpstart. In 2010, she'll move to her own condo in Nashville.

5. Lawrence, Kansas: Taylor visits her best friend, Abigail Anderson, at The University of Kansas.

6. Los Angeles: Taylor visits her friends Miley Cyrus and Selena Gomez here regularly; she's also stayed in the L.A. home of Tim McGraw and Faith Hill.

7. Evansville, Indiana: The location of Taylor's first concert of her *Fearless* Tour.

8. Boise, Idaho: Taylor was here the first time a fan recognized her in public.

9. New York: Taylor has performed multiple times here, from Madison Square Garden to *Saturday Night Live*, where she served as both host and musical guest.

10. Las Vegas: Taylor appeared as "Haley" on an episode of *CSI Las Vegas*, which is set in the city known for its casinos.

Chapter Seven

What's Up, Taylor?

The year 2009 could not have been better for Taylor Swift; she certainly ended the year with a bang. In November 2009, she took home all four of the Country Music Awards she was nominated for, including Entertainer of the Year. Taylor said winning that coveted award was her best moment of 2009. "Being on stage, accepting the CMA Entertainer of the Year award and getting to call my band up on stage, to have all of us up there, was really a fun and special moment for me that I won't forget," she told *People* magazine.

Less than two weeks later, Taylor won big at the American Music Awards. One of her five awards was for Artist of the Year, which Taylor nabbed from other favorites like Michael Jackson, Eminen, Lady Gaga, and Kings of Leon. Taylor, who won an AMA in 2008 for Best Female Country Artist, considered the award a huge honor. "They are fan-voted and that's where I base most of my pride in awards," Taylor said. "Those are the ones that I'm most fond of because the fans went online and voted."

Taylor wrapped up November 2009 by playing two concerts of her *Fearless* Tour in England, the last of her sold-out concerts for the year. A slew of other honors soon followed. In December 2009, the *Associated Press* named Taylor Entertainer of the Year, and *Billboard* named her Artist of the Year. That same month, her second album, *Fearless*, went five times platinum.

December 2009 was a month of not only professional celebrations, but personal ones as well. On December 13, 2009, Taylor turned 20 years old. She could no longer call herself a teenager.

Happy Birthday, Happy Winter

So how did Taylor celebrate the big 2-0? Like past years, she hosted a Christmas–themed birthday party. Since her birthday falls in the weeks before the holiday, Taylor always turns her birthday into a second Christmas. "It's more like an end-of-year Christmas party that happens to be on my birthday," explained Taylor, who prepared butter and gingerbread cookies, topped with cream-cheese icing for the shindig.

Instead of going to a fancy restaurant, Taylor chose to spend her 20th birthday at home, surrounded by her family, friends, band, and tour crew. Because home is such an important aspect of Taylor's life, it's no surprise the biggest birthday gift was from Taylor to her former schools. In honor of her special day, Taylor gave $250,000 dollars to schools she either attended or with which she had a connection.

"Something I wanted to do at the end of this amazing year and especially on my birthday was give back to something I really believe in, which is education," said Taylor. "The schools that I went to and the amazing people I got to learn from really turned me into who I am, and I wanted to give back."

Taylor donated money to these Nashville area schools: Hendersonville High School, Ellis Middle School, and Pope John Paul II High School. The Wyomissing Area School District in Pennsylvania was also a recipient. The district received $25,000 toward teacher's salaries, books and educational programs. The school board was pleased with the donation. "It just speaks to Taylor's character as a young woman," said Angel L. Helm, a school board member. "She's awesome."

After her birthday, Taylor spent Christmas 2009 at home with her family. Taylor loves the winter; it's her favorite time of year. The Swift house is

At the 2010 Grammys, Taylor sang a duet with legendary singer-songwriter, Stevie Nicks of Fleetwood Mac.

always full of holiday spirit come December, thanks to Taylor's mom, Andrea, who decorates so much she "makes the house look like the North Pole," Taylor said.

There's no other place Taylor wants to be come the holidays than home. Returning to Hendersonville after being in Los Angeles for three weeks, Taylor enjoyed seeing the sights and sounds of the season as the year 2009 neared its end. "There were cars jammed into every last parking spot available," she said, describing her hometown. "I could see the smoke billowing out of fireplace chimneys into cold winter air. It's the holidays. People are coming together and going out for dinner and something about seeing that just stuck with me. I love everything about this time of year, but mostly the way that people find ways to be with the ones they love. And I love sweaters. Everyone is wearing sweaters right now."

But Christmas 2009 was also bittersweet. "My brother's leaving for college next year, and I'm moving out in a few months," she told *Rolling Stone*. "So this was sort of a moment in time for me. I was definitely recording all of it in my mind, the last Christmas with all of us being in the same place."

Taylor even tweeted about the impact of that future move from her parent's house into her own place. "The last Christmas with all of us under one roof, how weird is that?" she wrote. "Merry Christmas to you guys, hug your families."

New Year, New Honors

Taylor spent New Year's Eve 2010 as casually as she did her birthday and Christmas. She had dinner with friend Hayley Williams of Paramore and then went home. In fact, she was texting Hayley when the year changed.

Taylor sent Hayley a note "to let her know I got home from dinner, and that my paranoid thoughts of getting in a car wreck were unwarranted," she said. After finishing

Home **Sweet Home**

■ Although Taylor bought a Nashville condo in the fall of 2009, she still hadn't moved into it by the beginning of 2010. That's because she was having fun fixing it up to be a magical place, almost a fairytale world.

In October 2009, on *The Oprah Winfrey Show*, Taylor said she wanted her new place to boast an "Old World, eclectic feel." She also said she was considering bright colors, draping fabrics, and "a different knob on every cabinet." And, perhaps to show she's still a kid at heart, she said she wanted a tree house in her living room, as well as a pond. "It's going to be my fantasy world," she told *Rolling Stone*. "The pond is a moat around my fireplace and may possibly have Koi fish in it. "

To make her penthouse condo even more magical, Taylor planned to have stepping stones in the pond, which would lead to a spiral staircase. The staircase would wind up to a human size birdcage, and inside the birdcage, would be a telescope for viewing stars on her faux night sky ceiling.

up the text, which read "Don't worry about me; I'm not dead," Taylor peeked at the clock. "I actually got to experience looking at the clock when it struck midnight, and that was a really fun moment for me," she said. "It was the most unconventional New Year's Eve I've ever had."

Like New Year's Eve, January 2010 was a laid-back month for Taylor. Without concerts or any major appearances, Taylor was free to take walks, snap photos, and think. She also participated in two charitable events. She performed at and supported the *Hope for Haiti Now* global telethon to raise funds for the impoverished country devastated by an earthquake. She also attended "An Unforgettable Evening" benefiting the Entertainment Industry Foundation's (EIF) Women's Cancer Research Fund.

The month was also full of honors and surprises for the singer-songwriter. According to Nielsen SoundScan, Taylor sold 4,643,000 digital units in 2009 alone. The only person to sell more digital songs in 2009 was Michael Jackson. Despite the King of Pop's reign at the top of digital downloads for the year, Taylor was named the top-selling digital artist in music history. By January 2010, Taylor had sold over 24.3 million digital songs. Also in January, Taylor attended the People's Choice awards, where she took home the award for Favorite Female Artist.

All of these honors led up to the biggest night in Taylor's career thus far: the 2010 Grammys. At the end of 2009, Taylor—nominated for eight Grammy awards—said winning a Grammy would be at the top of her list of things to do in 2010. "That would be something I would never forget," she said.

Taylor had been nominated for a Grammy in 2008 for Best New Artist, but lost to Amy Winehouse. In 2009, she performed at the Grammys with Miley Cyrus,

happens in L.A."

Taylor arrived at the 2010 Grammys with her mom. She wore a midnight blue, sparkly Franco Kaufman dress. And it wasn't long before Taylor showed off the gown on stage. Although she did not win Song or Record of the Year, she won Best Country Album. This was her first televised award of the night, as she won Best Female Country Vocal Performance and Best Country Song, both for "White Horse," off stage in a special ceremony.

Upon claiming her Grammy for Best Country Album, Taylor said, "This is my first time walking up those stairs to accept a Grammy on national television." She immediately thanked her label, Big Machine Records, for allowing her to write all of her own songs. The moment was unbelievable for Taylor. "I just keep thinking back to like when you're in 2nd grade and you sing at your talent show for the first time and people joke around and they say 'oh maybe we'll see you at the

Fearless Tour, Take Two

■ Taylor did not get much time to sit around and savor her big win at the 2010 Grammys. She soon headed off to Australia to start the second leg of her *Fearless* tour. Of course, Taylor didn't mind. Performing live in concert is something she loves to do. She has fine memories of her 2009 tour. "I'm gonna think back to those moments standing on that stage, hearing that incredible crowd noise come at me," Taylor said. "The screaming that happened on that tour from the crowd was at a volume level I have never experienced before. Those are definitely the moments I'll remember when I need a pick me up."

More of those amazing fan moments came when Taylor performed in Australia throughout February before heading to the States in March for shows in 29 cities, from Tampa to Detroit to Washington, D. C., The second leg of her *Fearless* Tour was set to run through June 2010. All of the shows sold out within minutes, something she did not take for granted.

"I've never expected that kind of success," she said, according to MTV. "I've never felt entitled to my show selling out or things like this happening to me, but the fact that they've happened to me has been wonderful."

but was not been nominated for any awards. The 2010 Grammys were special, in that Taylor was not only nominated for major awards like Album of the Year, but she was also set to perform her song "Today was a Fairytale" from the *Valentine's Day* soundtrack. Taylor didn't go into the night with any expectations or predictions. "You never know what's going to happen," she said before the award show. "I like being nominated for eight, I'm not going to lie. I like that feeling. It makes me smile. All I know is that I'm a really, really happy person, thinking about being nominated for eight of them, and I think that's a gift in itself, so we'll see what

Grammys someday' but that just seems like an impossible dream," she said. "I just feel like I'm standing here accepting an impossible dream right now."

The 2010 Grammys were full of spectacular live performances, including one by Taylor. Radio show personality Ryan Seacrest introduced Taylor's performance that night with much affection. "There is so much I could say about this next woman and all of it is good," Ryan said. "If you've listened to her lyrics, you know this remarkably gifted singer-songwriter tells her own story better than anyone else ever could. The truth is you could not make up a success story like this one.

Taylor and Pink were both nominated for Best Female Pop Vocal Performance at the 2010 Grammys.

After learning she won Album of the Year at the 2010 Grammys, a surprised Taylor Swift made eye contact with her mom and best friend, Andrea Swift.

And now that story continues."

After Taylor sang a shortened version of "Today was a Fairytale," she was joined on stage by legendary singer Stevie Nicks of Fleetwood Mac fame. Taylor and Stevie sang a duet of "Rhiannon," a song written by Stevie and made famous by Fleetwood Mac in the late 1970s. The two ended the performance with a changed up version of "You Belong With Me" that had a folky, almost Hawaiian sound. Stevie Nicks sang backup and played tambourine. At the end of the performance, Taylor and Stevie hugged.

The night ended on a high note for Taylor. She won Album of the Year for *Fearless*, beating out albums by Beyonce, Black Eyed Peas, Lady Gaga, and Dave Matthews Band. Taylor seemed both shocked and humbled by the coveted award. "I just hope that you know how much this means to me and to Nathan, my producer, and to all these musicians you see on this stage, that we get to take this back to Nashville," said Taylor, who noted her dad and brother were probably at home "freaking out" in the living room

Taylor thanked her father for his support of her musical interests. "Thank you for all those times that you said I could do whatever I wanted in life," she said. She also thanked her mother, whom she called her "best friend."

Taylor knew even then that winning a Grammy would be an unforgettable moment in her life. "When we're 80 years old and we're telling the same stories over and over again to our grandkids, and they're so annoyed with us," she explained "This is the story we are going to be telling over and over again: in 2010, that we got to win Album of the Year at the Grammys. Thank you, thank you, thank you."

Valentine's Day

On February 12, while Taylor was playing a concert in Adelaide, Australia, the film *Valentine's Day* was opening at home. The Garry Marshall directed film boasted a star-studded cast, including Jessica Alba, Kathy Bates, Jessica Biel, Bradley Cooper, Eric Dane, Patrick Dempsey, Hector Elizondo, Jamie Foxx, Jennifer Garner, Topher Grace, Anne Hathaway, Ashton Kutcher, Queen Latifah, Taylor Lautner, George Lopez, Shirley Maclaine, Emma Roberts, and Julia Roberts. It was Taylor's onscreen acting debut.

The romantic comedy was about multiple, inter-connected love stories, all pertaining to Valentine's Day. One storyline was about a florist who proposes to his girlfriend. Another was about a woman who throws an "I hate Valentine's Day" party. And yet another plotline dealt with a teen babysitter looking for advice about first love.

In the movie, Taylor played Felicia, an outspoken, popular prom queen type who is dating the equally popular jock. "I play the kind of girl I didn't like in high school," Taylor said of her character. "She's forced to go to gym class and doesn't want to be there." In the film, Felicia and her boyfriend, Willy, played by *New Moon* star Taylor Lautner, get interviewed for a local L.A. television station's segment on love. "Oh my gosh, I totally love him," Felicia said during the segment, hugging Willy. "See, he even wrote his number on my hand."

The two proceeded to kiss heavily in front the camera, and the segment is almost sickening to the reporter. "There you have it—young love," he said, "Full of promise, full of hope, ignorant of reality."

Most of the Taylor and Taylor scenes took place on a high school track/football field. Taylor wore a gym-class uniform, red shorts, and a grey T-shirt. In one scene, the two Taylors were surrounded by the heart shape formation of the school's marching band.

Filming the movie was a blast for Taylor. She not only started a brief romance with her onscreen boyfriend, Taylor Lautner, but she also got along well with her first director. "Garry Marshall was wonderful," Taylor told *The New York Times Style Magazine*. "And both of our lucky numbers are 13, so we talked about that most of the time."

The number 13 appears in the film; it's the number Willy wrote on Felicia's hand. Taylor considers the number lucky because her birthday is December 13. The number has also played a role in many big moments of her life. "I played on Jay Leno on February 13th. My album went gold in 13 weeks, the CMT voting for breakthrough video of the year stopped on April 13th," she explained. "When I was at the CMT awards, my record label had a row of seats arranged and they didn't know what row it was going to be, and when they got there…the ticket said that they were in letter M, which is the thirteenth letter, and my record label president's seat number was seat 13."

There were a few confusing moments during the filming, especially since there were two Taylors on set. Taylor Swift soon found a way to fix the problem.

"All of the production guys kept saying, 'Taylor, on your mark—no, not you, Taylor—no, the other Taylor—not that one, the other,'" she explained. "So halfway through the day, I was like, OK look, call him, 'Taylor,' and call me, 'Swifty.' Confusion solved."

In honor of Valentine's Day, Taylor appeared on the February/March cover of *Girl's Life* wearing a cupid-inspired outfit and heart-shaped locket. The article featured her advice for love and how to handle that time of year. "I typically don't ever have a boyfriend on Valentine's Day. I see it as an opportunity to just hang out with my other single girlfriends," she said. "Being single is something that I have never looked at as being a curse. It's that time for you to figure out what you like and how you like to spend time by yourself."

The film wasn't just an acting credit for Taylor, but a musical credit, too. Her original song "Today Was a Fairytale" appeared on the movie's soundtrack. In January, before the movie was even released, the song sold more than 325,000 downloads in its first week. The tune made music history; it was the fastest selling download by a female artist.

Album Number Three

After falling in love with Taylor's first and second albums, as well as her special edition LPs, Taylor's fans are eagerly awaiting the release of her third album. Although no specific release date has been mentioned, the album will likely be out by the end of 2010. "I like to have two years in between albums," Taylor explained. "So if you take *Fearless* and go forward two years, that's my ideal place to put out the next record, because I think two years of growth and development and feelings and life intake, love intake, emotion output, is my preferred formula for albums right now."

By the end of 2009, Taylor said she'd already written most of the songs for the third album and had recorded about half of them. She even tweeted about her recording sessions: "More recording. So excited. So excited. So excited. See, I said that three times. Once for every album we've made in this studio."

Taylor has given a few clues as to what kind of songs will be featured on her next record. First, she wants it to outdo her first two albums. "Hopefully, when the third album comes out, I'll be even more proud of it than anything I've put out before," she said backstage at *The Oprah Winfrey Show*. She said her inspiration for the songs on the third album came from Keith Urban and John Mayer." I'm inspired by people who I feel know exactly who they are, and that inspires me to continue to figure out and inform who I am as an artist," she added.

The songs on the next album will likely reflect her life experiences, and may even represent the changes in her life as she enters her 20s. "Vulnerability and honesty are themes in my music," she said. "I don't know what vulnerability looks like at 20, but I'm sure I'll find out."

Though she may try out new sounds on her third album, she never wants to alienate her fans. "I don't ever want to put out an album that was like 'my personal album' that, you know, no one can relate to, but I personally can relate to," she told GACtv. "Cause I just really, really always want to consider the 14-year-old girl who's driving home and just got broken up with at school, and she's like so upset so she needs to put in the CD. I want a song on the album for her. And I want a song on the album for this other girl that I met over here. And I want a song on the album for this guy who told me this life story. It's always going to be about the fans, and I hope that never changes."

There are a handful of Taylor Swift songs, some only available on iTunes and YouTube, that have never officially been released on any specific album. These include "I'd Lie," "Permanent Marker," "Sparks Fly," and "Your Anything." Could these songs appear on Taylor's third album? Unfortunately, Taylor fans will just have to wait and see.

There's always room for surprises, though.

"I think that it's fun making an album," Taylor told *Rolling Stone*. "Knowing that two days before you're scheduled to have the last master in, and everything is finished, and they're about to go print up the booklets, I can write something, call up my producer, we can get in the studio, put a rush on it, get an overnight mix, and that can be a last-minute addition to the record. I've had that happen on both my first and second album; the last-minute, 11th-hour songs."

Without releasing the titles of any of the songs, Taylor did give a hint about one particular tune. Remember how Taylor once wrote a song on a paper towel at the airport?

"I think I'm going to put (that song) on my third record," she divulged. "So stay tuned."

Stay tuned is right. With four Grammy wins, an acting gig, and a third album on its way, there seems to be no end to the Taylor Swift success story. Like a good album, it's sure to play on and on and on.

Taylor **Squared**

■ What happens when two young, good-looking stars with the same exact first name start dating? It's a story people and celebrity magazines can't stop talking about.

Such was the case with Taylor Swift and Taylor Lautner, 17, who met and eventually started dating after playing onscreen boyfriend and girlfriend in the film *Valentine's Day*.

The two were soon spotted and photographed many times by the paparazzi. One time, they were caught eating frozen yogurt together. It was rumored the two were an item, though neither confirmed nor denied the idea. Taylor hinted at dating the *New Moon* hunk during her monologue on *Saturday Night Live* in November 2009. A few weeks later, when Taylor Lautner hosted the show, he beat up a cardboard cut out of Kanye West during his monologue. It was a re-imagination of the MTV VMAs.

By December 29, after a three-month courtship, the two Taylors broke up. According to *Us Magazine* sources, the relationship was not as serious as the media made it out to be. The two Taylors decided they would be better off as friends. Some sources said Taylor Lautner liked Taylor Swift more than she liked him; that he often traveled to see her but she did not do the same for him.

Post Taylor Lautner, where is Taylor's love life heading? Well, after the Grammys, photos of Taylor and Cory Monteith of *Glee* were posted on celebrity websites and blogs. The two were seen together at a pre-Grammy party hosted by Clive Davis and a few days earlier inside Jerry's Deli.

Although rumors soon spread about a possible relationship between Taylor and Cory, music will always be her first passion until she meets the guy who knocks her socks off. Meanwhile, she won't go looking for love.

"I don't look for boyfriends," Taylor said. "I don't really scour the awards shows for who I'm going to date, but I think love happens when you're not looking for it, and when it happens, I'm not going to be the one to overthink it."

The Ultimate Taylor Swift **Quiz**

Think you know everything about Taylor Swift? Take this quiz and find out if you're a FAN, a SUPER FAN, or a card-carrying member of TEAM TAYLOR.

The Real Taylor Swift

Answer the following multiple-choice questions:

1. What is the one beverage Taylor always keeps in her refrigerator?
A. Grape juice
B. Chocolate milk
C. Cola
D. Orange juice

2. What is the one cosmetic Taylor can't live without?
A. Bronzer
B. Black eyeliner
C. Lip gloss
D. Moisturizer

3. What food did Taylor call her "guilty pleasure"?
A. Pancakes
B. Chocolate chips
C. Peanut butter
D. Whip cream

4. What did Taylor call her "dorky little secret"?
A. She eats peanut butter right out of the jar
B. She listens to her own CDs before bed
C. She wears a belt with every outfit
D. She wears a retainer at night

5. Why is Taylor happy about having long arms?
A. So she can reach the top shelf at the grocery store
B. So she can take great MySpace pictures

C. So she can hug two people at once
D. So she can touch her toes

6. What henna tattoo did Taylor have on the bottom of her foot?
A. A butterfly
B. A heart
C. Angel's wings
D. A 'T' for Taylor

7. Which of the following is NOT one of the career fields Taylor has considered?
A. Forensic Science
B. Business
C. Advertising
D. Cosmetology

8. How many auto accidents has Taylor been in?
A. One
B. Two
C. Three
D. None

9. Taylor sang back up vocals for the song "Two is Better than One" by which band?
A. Boys like Girls
B. Kings of Leon
C. Love and Theft
D. Def Leppard

10. Which Jennifer did Taylor say she admired for her "composure and grace"?
A. Jennifer Aniston
B. Jennifer Lopez
C. Jennifer Hudson
D. Jennifer Garner

11. While Taylor was singing "You're Not Sorry" during her *Fearless* tour, who popped out of her piano for a prank?
A. Kellie Pickler

B. Andrea Swift
C. Taylor's cat
D. Caitlin Evanson

12. Who was the only star to sell more digitally downloaded songs than Taylor in 2009?
A. Michael Jackson
B. Janet Jackson
C. Beyonce Knowles
D. Miley Cyrus

13. What is Taylor's favorite time of year?
A. Winter
B. Spring
C. Summer
D. Fall

14. Taylor arrived at the 2009 MTV Video Music Awards in a what?
A. Limo
B. Horse-drawn carriage
C. Fire engine
D. Police escort

15. What is one of Taylor's favorite hobbies?
A. Sewing
B. Scrapbooking
C. Baking
D. Collecting bottle caps

16. Which director gave Taylor a signed copy of a screenplay to one of his movies?
A. James Cameron
B. Steven Spielberg
C. Robert Zemeckis
D. Richard Curtis

17. What is Taylor's favorite watermelon flavored candy?
A. Jolly Ranchers
B. Now and Laters
C. Sour Patch Kids
D. Nerds

18. What is the first thing Taylor needs to do in the morning?
A. Drink coffee
B. Take a shower
C. Yoga
D. Put in her contacts

19. Taylor's family owns two dogs of what breed?
A. West Highland Terriers
B. Doberman Pinschers
C. Golden Retrievers
D. Black Labs

20. Which of the following boys did Taylor NOT have a crush on?
A. Chace Crawford
B. Justin Timberlake
C. Taylor Hanson
D. Brad Pitt

21. When pranking Keith Urban, which member of Kiss did Taylor dress up as?
A. The Demon
B. Spaceman
C. Starchild
D. Catman

22. What is Taylor's signature hand gesture?
A. Peace sign
B. Heart
C. OK sign
D. Thumbs up

23. What did Taylor do with her old Jessica McClintock prom dress?
A. She donated it to charity
B. She gave it to best friend, Abigail
C. She wore it again for an award show
D. She reused it to make sofa pillows

24. What does Taylor like to dip her French fries into?

A. Ketchup
B. Mustard
C. Mayonnaise
D. Chocolate shake

25. What was Taylor's favorite book in grade school?
A. *The Adventures of Huckleberry Finn* by Mark Twain
B. *To Kill a Mockingbird* by Harper Lee
C. *The Diary of Anne Frank*
D. *Where the Red Fern Grows* by Wilson Rawls

Answer Key:

Give yourself one point for every question you answered correctly.

Answers:
1. A
2. B
3. D
4. D
5. B
6. B
7. D
8. C
9. A
10. C
11. A
12. A
13. A
14. B
15. C
16. D
17. C
18. A
19. B
20. D
21. B
22. B
23. A
24. D
25. B

What does your score mean?

* If you got 10-16 questions correct, you're a Taylor Swift FAN. You boast a good base knowledge of the country and pop superstar but have probably just discovered Taylor and her music.

* If you got 17-21 questions correct, you're a SUPER FAN. You must read her blog and fan sites often, because you know Taylor really well, like a sister.

* If you got 22-25 correct, you're a true member of TEAM TAYLOR. You deserve front row tickets to her concert, since you know Taylor almost as much as she knows herself!

December 1989: Taylor Alison Swift was born December 13 to Scott and Andrea Swift in Wyomissing, Pennsylvania.

March 1982: Taylor's brother, Austin, is born.

January 1996: LeAnn Rimes released her debut album; Taylor heard the song "Blue" at age six and fell in love with country music.

1999-2000: In fourth grade, Taylor wrote "Monster in My Closet," a three-page poem that won a national poetry contest.

June 2000: At age 10, Taylor sang karaoke for the first time at Henny's Restaurant in Stone Harbor, New Jersey.

March 2001: During spring break, Taylor popped into record labels on Nashville's Music Row with the pitch: "Hey, I'm 11 and I want a record deal. Call me."

August 2002: Taylor sang the National Anthem at the US Open Tennis Tournament in New York. There, she was discovered by Dan Dymtrow, manager for Britney Spears.

September 2002: Taylor opened for The Charlie Daniels Band at The Pat Garrett Roadhouse in Strausstown, Pennsylvania.

September 2003: Taylor signed a development deal with RCA Records.

January 2004: Taylor wrote what would be her first published song, "The Outside."

April 2004: After being offered a songwriting job with Sony/ATV, Taylor moved to Hendersonville, Tennessee, to pursue a career in country music in nearby Nashville.

August 2004: Taylor appeared in *Vanity Fair* as well as the Abercrombie & Fitch catalog, as part of a "Rising Stars" campaign; Taylor's original song "The Outside" appeared on the Maybelline *Chicks with Attitude* compilation CD, which coincided with a summer concert tour featuring Liz Phair; Taylor started her freshman year at Hendersonville High School and met her best friend, Abigail Anderson, in English class.

Winter/Spring 2005: Taylor wrote and performed "Our Song" for the ninth grade talent show at HHS.

Summer 2005: Taylor played a songwriters' showcase at The Bluebird Café in Nashville and was discovered by Scott Borchetta, who signed her to his new label, Big Machine Records.

August 2005: Taylor played "Tim McGraw" for Scott Borchetta, and he immediately knew the song would be her first single.

November 2005: Taylor wrote her first archived blog entry on MySpace.

June 2006: Taylor's first single, "Tim McGraw," was released.

October 2006: Taylor's first album, *Taylor Swift*, was released

November 2006: Taylor opened for Rascall Flatts on tour.

January 2007: George Strait invited Taylor to open for his arena tour.

February 2007: Taylor's tune "Our Song" was released as a single.

March 2007: "Teardrops on My Guitar" was released.

April 2007: Taylor joined Brad Paisley's *Bonfire & Amplifiers* Tour as an opening act, along with Kellie Pickler and Jack Ingram; Taylor won Breakthrough Video of the Year for "Our Song" at the Country Music Television (CMT) Awards.

May 2007: Taylor met Tim McGraw in person at the Academy of Country Music (ACM) Awards.

June 2007: Taylor's self-titled album went platinum with sales totaling one million.

July 2007: Taylor performed in the Country Music Association (CMA) Music Festival: "Country's Night to Rock" on ABC; Taylor opened for Tim McGraw and Faith Hill for their Soul2Soul Tour.

October 2007: Taylor's Christmas album *Sounds of the Season: The Taylor Swift Holiday Collection* was released; The pop version of "Teardrops on My Guitar" was released; Taylor won the Nashville Songwriter's Association International Songwriter/Artist of the Year, an honor she shared with Alan Jackson.

November 2007: Taylor won a BMI award for writing "Tim McGraw;" Taylor won the Horizon Award at the CMA Awards.

December 2007: Taylor was nominated for Best New Artist at the Grammy Awards

January 2008: Taylor released *Live from Soho: Taylor Swift*, an iTunes exclusive album she recorded at the Apple store in the Soho neighborhood of New York City.

March 2008: Taylor joined Kenny Chesney's *Keg in the Closet* Tour.

April 2008: Taylor's self-titled album went triple platinum; Taylor won Video of the Year and Female Video of the Year at the CMT Awards.

May 2008: Taylor took home the award for Top New Female Vocalist at the ACM Awards.

July 2008: Taylor released *Beautiful Eyes*, a Wal-Mart exclusive album.

September 2008: Taylor's song "White Horse" was featured on an episode of *Grey's Anatomy*; Taylor's song "Love Story" was released.

October 2008: Taylor sang the National Anthem for Game Three of the World Series, which the Philadelphia Phillies won; Taylor performed on an episode of CMT's *Crossroads* with Def Leppard, her mom's favorite band.

November 2008: "Teardrops on my Guitar" was named Country Song of the Year at the BMI Awards; Taylor won Favorite Female Artist/Country at the American Music Awards (AMA); Taylor released her sophomore album, *Fearless* and it debuted at No. 1 on the Billboard Top 200 albums; during her album release party on *The Ellen DeGeneres Show*, Taylor talked about her break up with Joe Jonas for the first time.

December 2008: Nielsen Sound-Scan named Taylor Swift the best-selling artist of 2008.

January 2009: Taylor was the youngest country musical guest to perform on *Saturday Night Live*; Taylor launched her L.E.I. sundress line at Wal-Mart.

February 2009: Taylor appeared in *Jonas Brothers: The 3D Concert Experience*; Taylor performed "Fifteen" with Miley Cyrus at the Grammy Awards; Taylor made the cover of *Rolling Stone* magazine.

March 2009: Taylor appeared on an episode of *CSI Las Vegas*; she played Haley, a rebellious teen whose parents own a motel.

April 2009: Taylor made a cameo performance of the song "Crazier" in *Hannah Montana: The Movie*; Taylor launched her 2009 *Fearless* Tour, with a first concert in Evansville, Indiana; Taylor won Album of the Year for *Fearless* at the ACM Awards; Taylor's single "You Belong With Me" was released.

September 2009: Taylor won Female Video of the Year at the MTV Video Music Awards (VMAs) but rapper Kanye West interrupted her acceptance speech; Taylor exceeded ten million in record sales.

October 2009: Taylor released her *Fearless Platinum Edition* album.

November 2009: Taylor served as both host and musical guest on *Saturday Night Live*; Taylor won four major awards, including Entertainer of the Year at the CMAs; Taylor won five awards at the AMAs, including Artist of the Year; According to Billboard, Taylor's self-titled album was named the longest charting album of the century.

December 2009: Taylor turned 20 years old; *Billboard* named Taylor Artist of the Year for 2009; *Fearless* was certified fives time platinum.

January 2010: Nielsen SoundScan named Taylor the top-selling digital artist in music history, with 24.3 million digital songs sold to date; *Billboard* named *Fearless* the best selling album of 2009; Taylor participated in the *Hope for Haiti* Now global telethon; Taylor's song "Today was a Fairytale" from the *Valentine's Day* soundtrack was named the fastest selling downloaded song by a female artist. Taylor won four Grammy awards, including Album of the Year for *Fearless*.

February 2010: Taylor began her 2010 *Fearless* Tour in Australia; Taylor made her acting debut in the star-studded film *Valentine's Day*, directed by Garry Marshall.

Spring 2010: Taylor's greeting card line with American Greetings is set to launch.

BIBLIOGRAPHY

Online & Print Articles

Bradley, Victoria. "Nineteen Now" *Whirl* Dec. 2008.

Bried, Erin. "Taylor Swift has 1,056,375 friends." *Self* Mar. 2009: 44-46.

Cabral, Elizabeth and Elio Iannacci. "Fearless & Fabulous." *Flare* June 2009: 112-142.

Caramanica, John. "A Young Outsider's Life…" *The New York Times* 5 Sept. 2008.

Clark, Larry Wayne. "Taking the 'Backward' Approach with Liz Rose." (Originally appeared in *Music Row* magazine) 2006.

Cook, Katie. "Taylor Swift: CMT Insider Interview, Part 1/2." *CMT News* 26 Nov. 2008.

Corbett, Holly. "Taylor Swift: She won't run…" *Seventeen* May 2009: 108, 111-112.

Darden, Beville. "John Rich Talks Writing With Taylor Swift" *The Boot* 1 April 2009.

Darden, Beville. "Taylor Swift Collaborates…Colbie Caillat" *The Boot* 27 March 2008

Day, Rick. "10 Questions for Taylor Swift." *Time* 23 April 2009.

DeMara, Bruce. "Taylor Swift: Country music's rising star." *The Star* 12 Jan. 2008.

Evans, Rory. "Taylor Made." *Women's Health* Dec. 2008.

Freedom du Lac, J. "Taylor Swift… Kid in Country." *The Washington Post* 28 Feb. 2008.

Forr, Amanda. "Fabulously Fearless." *Girl's Life* Dec 2008/Jan. 2009: 50-52.

Finan, Eileen. "Guy Behind Taylor Swift Song Revealed." *People* 2 Dec. 2008.

Finan, Eileen. "5 Questions for Taylor Swift" *People* 2 Dec. 2008.

Geller, Wendy. "Taylor Swift inspires Christmas 'Swiftmas' Song." 10 Dec. 2009.

Grigoriadis, Vanessa. "Taylor Swift in Her Own Words" *Rolling Stone* 20 Feb. 2009

Grigoriadis, Vanessa. "The Very Pink, Very Perfect Life…" *Rolling Stone* 19 Feb. 2009.

Hansen, Amy Gail. "Taylor Swift: Love Story." *Triumph Books* 2009.

Harbin, Lee. "Lee Alumnus Nathan Chapman…" *The Chattanoogan* 9 Dec 2009.

Hirschburg, Lynn. "Little Miss Sunshine: Taylor Swift, Little Country Darlin…" *The New York Times Style Magazine* Holiday Issue 2009: 130-135.

Horner, Marianne. "Taylor Swift: Letting Her Hair Down." *Country Weekly* 12 Jan. 2009.

Jackson, Vincent. "No Longer an Outsider…" *The Press of Atlantic City* 2 Aug. 2004.

Kawashima, Dale. "Rising Country Star Taylor Swift…" *Songwriter Universe*.

King, Jackie Lee. "Taylor Swift: A Place in This World" *Unrated Magazine* July 2007.

Kotb, Hoda. "On tour with Taylor Swift" *Dateline NBC*, Transcript 31 May 2009.

MeKeel, David. "Taylor Swift Donates $25,000…" *The Reading Eagle* 12 Jan. 2010

Merkin, Daphne. "The Story Teller." *Allure* April 2009: 188-196.

Michel, Sia. "Miss Independent" *InStyle* Dec. 2009: 347-355.

Montes, Michael. "Musician Interview" *Florida Entertainment Scene* 17 July 2007

Morris, Edward. "…Liz Rose SESAC's Songwriter of the Year" *CMT News* 6 Nov. 2007.

Morris, Edward. "SESAC Honors Songwriter Liz Rose…" *CMT News* 29 Sept. 2009.

Ogara, Joe. "Taylor Swift Enjoys Sharing her Diaries." *Nuvo.* 13 Oct. 2009.

Paulson, Dave. "Nathan Barlowe talks…Taylor Swift" *The Tennessean* 24 Nov. 2009

Pellettieri, Cortney. "Taylor Swift: On My Mind." *InStyle* July 2009: 182.

Rasmussen, Tracy. "Berks native Taylor Swift's…" *Reading Eagle* 8 Feb. 2008.

Rech, Debra. "Hitting a High Note…" *The Press of Atlantic City* 21 Aug. 2002.

Rosen, Jody. "Taylor Swift: Little Miss Perfect" *Blender* 6 March 2008.

Rosenberg, Carissa. "…This Girl is Singing Your Song." *Seventeen* June 2008: 98-101.

Roznovsky, Lindsey. "Taylor Swift's Fascination/Fairy Tale." *CMT News* 10 Nov. 2008.

Sandell, Laurie. "Taylor Swift: Bomb-Shell in Blue Jeans." *Glamour* 1 July 2009.

Sanz, Cynthia. "Taylor Swift Gives Big as She Turns 20." *People* 14 Dec. 2009.

Scaggs, Austin. "Taylor's Time: Catching up…" *Rolling Stone* 25 Jan. 2010.

Scaggs, Austin. "The Unabridged Taylor Swift." *Rolling Stone* 2 Dec. 2008.

Spatz, David J. "Stone Harbor's Very Own…" *The Seven Mile Times*. July 2008: 14-16.

Strauss, Robert. "Taylor Swift's Stone Harbor." *The Philadelphia Inquirer* 15 May 2009.

Taylor Swift: The Phenomenon." *Cosmo Girl* Dec. 2008/Jan. 2009: 101-105.

Tucker, Ken. "Taylor Swift Goes Global." *Billboard* 25 Oct. 2008: 22-25.

Vadnal, Julie. "Women in Music: Taylor Swift." *Elle* 15 June 2009.

Vena, Jocelyn. "Taylor Swift Explains…13 is Her Lucky Number." *VH1* 7 May 2009.

Vena, Jocelyn. "Taylor Swift Announces New Leg of Fearless Tour." *MTV* 8 Oct. 2009.

Waterman, Laura. "Swift Ascent." *Teen Vogue* March 2009.

Williams, Karen L., Editor In Chief. *Life Story: Taylor Swift*, Bauer Publishing Company L.P. Aug. 2009.

Willman, Chris. "American Girl." *Entertainment Weekly* 8 Feb. 2008: 40-43.

Willman, Chris. "Swift Rise." *Entertainment Weekly* 20 Sept. 2009.

Wynne, Vincent. "Kings of Leon Producer Angelo Petraglia." *Gibson* 18 Aug. 2008.

"20 Question with Taylor Swift" *CMT News* 12 Nov. 2007.

Data, Images & Video Clips Accessed at the Following Websites:

www.associatedcontent.com
www.bestbuy.inc.com
www.bigmachinerecords.com
http://blogs.gactv.com/gactv/askt-heartist/taylorswift/
http://blog.nielsen.com/nielsenwire
www.bmi.com
www.brettjames.com/
www.cbsnews.com
www.cmt.com
www.copperfieldmusic.com
http://www.countrystandardtime.com
www.disneydreaming.com
http://ellen.warnerbros.com
http://www.facebook.com
www.fresh.amazon.com
www.gactv.com
www.gossipteen.com
http://home.earthlink.net/~deankay/Brian_Dean_Maher2.html
www.johnrich.com/
www.msnbc.com
www.mtv.com
www.myspacc.com
www.myspace.com/taylorswift
www.nathanchapman.com
www.nytimes.com/pages/t-magazine/index.html
www.oprah.com
www.peermusic.com/artistpage/Robert_Ellis_Orrall.html
www.people.com
http://plantcity2.tbo.com
www.seventeen.com
www.taylorswift.com
www.theinsider.com
www.umpgnashville.com
www.usmagazine.com
http://video.aol.ca/video
www.wikipedia.com
www.youtube.com

Audio/Lyrics:

Swift, Taylor. *Taylor Swift*. Big Machine Records, 2006.

Swift, Taylor *Fearless*. Big Machine Records, 2008.

Interviews

Luyben, Sharon, former music teacher of Taylor Swift. Personal interview. 2 Sept. 2009.